Gerald Coulson

THE MASTERWORKS

G-ADFI
COULSON

Gerald Coulson

THE MASTERWORKS

John Blake

DAVID & CHARLES
Newton Abbot • London

ACKNOWLEDGEMENTS

The artist and author would like to thank
the following for their help in compiling this book:

Solomon & Whitehead (Guild Prints) Ltd;
Venture Prints; *Aeroplane Monthly*;
Sir Arthur Marshall OBE DL; Halcyon Gallery;
Richard Lucraft; John Jenkins;
Imperial War Museum, Duxford; David Shepherd OBE

British Library Cataloguing in Publication Data
Blake, John
Gerald Coulson: the masterworks.
1. English paintings. Coulson, Gerald
I. Title
759.2

ISBN 0–7153–9869–5

Typeset and designed by John Youé using a Macintosh system
and printed in Singapore by C.S.Graphics Pte Ltd
for David & Charles plc
Brunel House Newton Abbot Devon

Contents

COULSON

Foreword

David Shepherd

As I began my own career as an aviation artist, I naturally share Gerry's love of and affinity for aircraft and flight. Indeed, he goes one better than me; he actually flies the things!

I am sure that both Gerry and I can speak for all aviation artists when we say that you cannot even begin to paint aircraft unless you get the 'feel' for them, and this of course means flying. Those who have never flown have missed some of the most spectacularly beautiful sights in nature; massive thunderclouds climbing, for example, interminably into the heavens over Africa. But it does not all have to be dramatic. *Sunday Morning* is one of the most delightful aviation paintings coming from anyone's studio and is, I think, Gerry's finest work. I have actually flown in a Tiger myself, experienced the wonderful blast of fresh air in one's face and heard the singing in the wires — here is the real spirit of flight.

Gerry does not, of course, confine himself to aviation subjects, as this beautiful book shows so clearly. Indeed, I have never asked him, but I feel that he would not wish to be known simply as an aviation artist. I regard myself as a landscape artist — whether one is painting a portrait, an aviation subject, an elephant or a steam engine, this is all life and life is a landscape. Gerry, I feel sure, feels the same. Whether it is the early morning mists rising around stark elm trees, the quiet of a forest at midday, or the bleak mountains of Cumbria or Scotland, Gerry has a sympathetic 'feel' for his subject. It is all here admirably portrayed in paint and this book is a magnificent tribute to a fine artist.

David Shepherd

Gerald Coulson at work in his studio

Introduction

Gerald Coulson

Many years ago, as what one would describe as a 'gifted' enthusiast, I met and talked painting with a professional of world-wide renown. He told me that if a book was ever published of an artist's life and work, then that artist could be considered as having 'arrived'.

When I was contacted by David & Charles for this book to be published, my self-esteem knew no bounds. However, thinking about it and talking about it is one thing, but putting it all together is something else again. A great many words were to be put down and arranged to make interesting reading — and where were all the pictures going to come from?

As far as the text was concerned — for me the most challenging part — a writer had to be found with both flair and sound knowledge of similar interests. John Blake had to be the man for the job. When he kindly consented I knew we were in with a chance. I doubt if I could have tracked down as many as a dozen paintings to contribute; yet around seventy colour plates needed to be amassed. As luck would have it, a considerable number of my works over the last few years have been published as fine art prints, so my relief was considerable when I was informed by the publisher, Solomon & Whitehead, that they held suitable colour transparencies in their files. These were made available and assembled, thereby solving what would otherwise have been an impossible task.

I would like to believe the results will serve to encourage all who are fascinated, as I was in my youth, by the magical effects that can be obtained on flat canvas, and who are trying to emulate them. If you have not yet quite achieved the desired results, keep at it. With dedication it is possible, and I hope the following pages will help to inspire you.

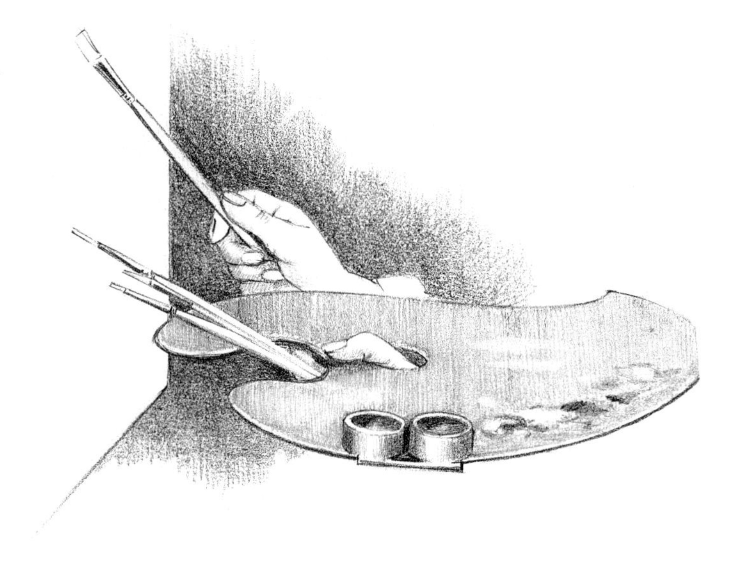

Presentation of a print of Quiet Forest *to the artist after sales passed the half million mark. From left to right: the chairman of Solomon & Whitehead, Jim Kearns, with financial director Graham Jones and Coulson*

THE LIFE AND TIMES OF

Gerald Coulson

Gerald Coulson is probably best known to the majority of people as the author of a long series of highly successful prints issued by Solomon and Whitehead. He has been with them for a long time, now — they first published him in 1976, and from then until the beginning of 1990 there have been around forty-seven unlimited and twenty limited editions. Almost all of these have been successes, beginning with *The Ploughman and the Sea, Winter Sunlight* and *Outbound Lancaster,* all of which reached the Top Ten in the Fine Arts Guild list in their first year. Another print, *Quiet Forest,* an unlimited edition, has sold over half a million copies — more than any other print Solomon and Whitehead have handled. None of their painters has ever sold better in the unlimited field than Gerald Coulson, and to mark the occasion of *Quiet Forest*'s half-million, they presented him with a copy autographed by a number of other artists: David Shepherd; his daughter Mandy Shepherd; Anthony Gibbs; Don Breckon; and Douglas West. The majority of the prints have been landscapes and aviation subjects, with one excursion into railway history in the painting of *Mallard* on her famous record-breaking run. The inclusion, from the very beginning, of aviation prints is not surprising when it is realised what a very large part flying has played, and continues to play, in Gerald's career. It has always loomed pretty large in his ideas, and he was never in any doubt but that his future career was to lie somewhere in aviation. By the time he was around eleven or twelve (he declines to be more precise), it had become his most absorbing interest. It was a time when the sky was beginning to show aeroplanes as a normal feature; a time of Royal Air Force expansion, in new types and new aerodromes; a time of new civil aircraft flying with Imperial Airways, British Airways and a large network of local air services.

This absorption in aviation continued to grow, threatening to take priority, as such things will, over more mundane matters of schoolwork — a problem familiar to all with any spark of spirit. Nor are such diversions confined to one's schooldays: the course notebooks of Rex Whistler, a young officer in the Welsh Guards during the war, still exist, embellished with sketches for the rococo designs that were to be his chief artistic legacy and including a superb baroque tank.

It was this interest in aircraft that started off Gerald Coulson's art career. He had not received — nor did he ever receive — any formal education or training in drawing and painting, and there was no previous trace of artistic ability in the family — though he must have inherited the more precise side of his talent, at least, from a father who designed and built classical and traditional furniture. It was his growing absorption with the shapes of aircraft that first fired him with the desire to express such things in pen or pencil, though only later that he began to think of enhancing these expressions in terms of added watercolour in background washes.

The initial fascination for drawing aeroplanes as well as just absorbing all the available information about them began quite simply, as it did for many others, in drawing wartime aircraft from photographs. Nothing from those early photo-copying days has survived (or possibly, been allowed to survive; not everybody wants to have his first tentative gropings towards perfection preserved to shame him before posterity, like those embarrassing photographs of babies on bearskin rugs).

Fastidiousness over accuracy and style was not long in manifesting itself, and it is permissible to believe that, whether he realised it himself or not, this was an early indication that his inclinations were going to take him into the engineering side of both civil aviation and Royal Air Force employment.

Some Early Influences

That period of the 1940s, when he was getting his first sight of the world of aviation art and was coming to grips with its problems, was also a period of great proliferation in boys' books on flying. And wrapped around these productions of the facile pens of W.E. Johns, Percy F. Westerman, Geo E. Rochester and dozens of others, were the bright dust jackets produced by aviation artists; furthermore it was a poor edition that did not boast a frontispiece, and superior, Christmas present-type books might contain up to half-a-dozen illustrations as well. It was a high point in the history of popular aircraft illustration, and one from which many future aviation artists of Gerald's age were to form their earliest ideas on the subject.

Curiously, he never seems to have been aware of any of these books and as many of the illustrations, mostly by Howard Leigh and Polish-born S.R. Drigin, would have made an angel weep, perhaps in his case it was no loss, although both artists were capable of good work on occasion. On the other hand John Hamilton, the London publishers responsible for many of the aviation books of the period, both fact and fiction, employed the gifted Stanley Orton Bradshaw for a lot of their work; besides using him as a book illustrator, they also produced several prints of his lively, colourful aircraft paintings. Bradshaw, be it noted, had the inestimable advantage of being a pilot himself (a fact that would have appealed to Gerald Coulson in later years) and flew with the Air Transport Auxiliary throughout World War II.

Although Gerald never, apparently, read any of these delectable books, he did see *Air Stories,* the classic pulp magazine of the late thirties which survived a few

Many of the aviation artists of the 1930s and 1940s were hard at work producing jackets and text illustrations for boys' fiction; World War II provided a wealth of material for writers and illustrators alike

months into World War II; a magazine that, if it employed Leigh and Drigin, also used the far greater talents of Geo. M. Blow, who combined an accurate eye and pen with a sympathy for mechanical objects akin to that of F. Gordon Crosby. It would appear that our hero really did exercise his talents and practise his skills as a draughtsman entirely on his own, with no discernible outside influence — well, not at that time, anyway.

But it was still aviation as a career first and drawing aeroplanes second; as he says himself quite firmly, the eventual alliance of aviation and art was largely the product of an inability to resist the sight of a sheet of white paper (something we have all suffered from, and many of us still do); an itch that contained no seed, no premonition of his future as a painter. Certainly at that time and for a good many years afterwards, the thought never entered his head that he might one day become a *professional artist.*

If he drew no inspiration from the pre-war aviation artists and illustrators, the situation changed entirely when, around the beginning of the war, he was introduced to that most celebrated of productions from the Studio presses, *How to Draw Planes* by Frank Wootton. Wootton did not become prominent specifically as a war artist until some time after the start of the war, the War Artists Committee being something of a cosy little club for established — and Establishment — figures, as concerned (at least initially) that approved professional artists should continue to earn a living as that the earth-shaking events in progress around them should be properly recorded. But besides being the author of the Studio publication, he had become famous, almost overnight, among aviation people and would-be aviation artists, through the prolific series of advertisements that he painted for de Havilland Propellers and other firms in the aircraft industry and which featured prominently in the pages of *Flight* and *The Aeroplane.* Fortunately for all of us, the Royal Air Force had very clear ideas as to what it wanted out of a war artist (recognisable aircraft, for a start) and in their indulgent hands Wootton went from strength to strength. Predictably, he also became Mr Coulson's inspiration as an artist.

Flight Refuelling Ltd

By now, the Coulson family were living in Malvern, Worcestershire, and here the initial link was forged that was to become a chain binding Gerald to aviation. Just down the road from the Coulsons lived Sir Alan Cobham, the great aerial adventurer, record-breaker and endless campaigner for an air-minded Britain in the 1920s and 1930s. On Saturday afternoons Gerald would help him in his garden and from this, and from his evident interest in aeronautical matters, came a design apprenticeship in Sir Alan's company, Flight Refuelling Ltd.

The company had been formed by Sir Alan before the war, largely to exploit commercially his well known pioneering work with in-flight refuelling, and culminating in his experiments for civil transatlantic flights in 1938 and 1939. However, all that had ceased with the war and Flight Refuelling had diversified heavily into a variety of aeronautical activities in order to stay alive.

On the outbreak of hostilities, they were comfortably established at Ford aerodrome on the south coast of England a few miles north of Littlehampton, where they had been since the days of Sir Alan's air circus, National Aviation Displays Ltd. From the end of 1937 they became tenants of the Air Ministry, who had bought the place, though they continued to occupy their hangars on the west side, sharing the aerodrome facilities with No 17 (Training) Group, Coastal Command. But in May 1939, Ford was handed over to the Admiralty, who set up the Royal Navy Observer School there and, finding the presence of all those civilians over on the other side something of an encumbrance, sent them packing.

So in May 1940 Flight Refuelling moved into the cloistered calm of the Morgan Motor Works at Malvern and there, in 1942, Gerald joined them, leaving school in order to do so. The company's move to Malvern, tedious though it must have been at the time, proved to be providential and timely, because on 18 August 1940 twenty-eight Ju 87s of II/StG77 evaded defending fighters and virtually destroyed everything in sight at Ford — including the Armstrong-Whitworth AW 23 and two Handley Page Harrow tankers of Flight Refuelling that were still stored there.

By the time Gerald Coulson joined the firm, he found them engaged in a very wide variety of research and development work. Bomber Command had been losing many aircraft because of icing during the severe winters of 1940 and 1941, and FR were developing systems for spreading de-icing fluid over wing leading edges (later replaced by ducted hot air inside the wing). Other work involved heated windscreens for aircraft; flame damping exhausts for night fighters, reducing the glare that ruined the pilot's night vision and could give him away to his target; self-sealing fuel tanks; and a remarkable scheme for supplying Spitfires and Hurricanes to Malta by towing them behind Wellingtons — which provided a sight in the skies around the Chilterns almost as odd as the occasional forays of the Gloster-Whittle jet from Stoke Orchard. The earliest flame-damping devices were crude, no more than flat plates fixed to the side of the cowling, shielding the fierce glare of the ejector exhausts from the pilot's eye. One of these may be seen on the Hurricane night fighter of No 85 Squadron depicted in Gerald's limited edition print *Hunter's Moon* (p70), issued in 1990.

Artistic Experiences

As far as his artistic talents were concerned at this stage of his career, Gerald was still concentrating on improving his drawing, which was a traditional and eminently sensible way of going about developing them. Outside the world of non-representational art, the saying that 'If you want to see how good a man is, look at his life drawing' is as true as ever it was, and Gerald was perfecting his own kind of life drawing at this time. He had not yet begun to get himself involved with colour, but very soon developed an interest in it, sparked off largely by the celebrated series of Wootton colour prints produced for the RAF Benevolent Fund, copies of which were displayed in the Drawing Office at Flight Refuelling. Using these as a basis, he started to analyse the artist's methods of texturing metal and fabric under various conditions of light.

He was still not contemplating a career as an artist, nor was he by any means fully converted to the use of colour, contenting himself for the most part with watercolour tinting of his pencil drawings. He was also drawing in charcoal (which Frank Wootton used to dramatically good effect), but found that, satisfactory although the medium undoubtedly was, the willow twigs from the garden, which were the only available form of charcoal, were irritating to use. However, the lean years of mid-war, when far more important things than artists' materials were in very short supply or non-existent, was really not the best of times to try and practise new media.

Eventually, of course, he bought his first box of oil paints and some suitable brushes and began to experiment — but, with no one available to explain how to go about it, it never occurred to him that the various pigments had to be toned down, rather than applied to the canvas absolutely raw from the tube (a condition in which, according to his recollections of the results, 'all the colours tended to look very much alike'). Study of some of Frank H. Mason's marine paintings might have convinced him that it was possible to get away with that sort of thing. He did get as far as painting two pictures under these far from promising conditions, but finding (hardly surprisingly) that he could not cope, he gave up the unequal struggle, returned to his previous mistress, the piece of charcoal, and continued where he had left off.

In all his efforts in pencil and charcoal so far, Gerald had been concentrating on getting the structure of the aircraft correct, and not really bothering to do anything to fill in the blank bits all round it. It now occurred to him that as all structures are basically the same, he should progress to something new and that there should be no problem, artistically speaking, in coping with trees, faces and landscape. This he discovered more or less to be true.

Composing a picture had never caused him the slightest trouble: 'You just fiddled about with the bits till they looked right'. Given a reasonably educated eye, this is really not at all a bad method. Many a first class professional will start operations on a painting by pushing around little bits of paper with aeroplanes or what-have-you drawn on them, on a large sheet of paper or a board; and unless you lack the ability or the inclination to trust everything to the Mk 1 eyeball or prefer to use more analytical and Euclidean methods, it seems to work pretty well. It has even been known for a submission for a Guild of Aviation Artists exhibition to be created by hawking a sketch of an aircraft about on an already created landscape until it looked as if it belonged . . .

These activities belonged to the period before he went into the Services, and it was only after Gerald had joined the Royal Air Force that he really began to consider skies and other background objects and how to treat them. By the time he was about to leave the Royal Air Force he had become really involved in representing the sky in his pictures; at this point he took up pastels — he was still quite firmly determined that he would never go back to oils — and was delighted with the results. He used the oil-bound, paper-covered variety, not the chalk ones, and discovered that the most splendid cloud effects could be obtained by grinding up the pastel to a powder and applying it with cotton wool. And then, after mastering the pastels, he screwed up his courage and went out and bought some hog hair brushes — and tried using oils again. And gave them up again.

After this he had a brilliant idea. It should be possible to combine watercolour with a suitable body medium such as process white and apply it with those otherwise useless hog hair brushes. Nobody told him how to do this; as in everything else in painting, he was, he says, completely self-taught and, with the exception of Frank Wootton's *How to Draw Planes,* had never bought any of the 'how-to-do-it' books. The discovery of water-colour mixed with white enchanted him. Nobody had told him about gouache.

Military Years

Gerald's military career did not turn out exactly as he had expected it to (few military careers ever do). He had wanted more than anything else to join the Royal Air Force but was thwarted in his attempt to become aircrew — only two out of the batch of fifty-two hopefuls at his Aircrew Selection Board in Birmingham were actually selected for flying training. So, desperate to get in at any cost, he opted for a ground trade. Within two hours of arriving at RAF Station Padgate he desperately wanted to go home again.

Having failed, through no fault of his own, to become a pilot he eventually found himself mustered as a technician. Although he had been trained as an apprentice engineer at Flight Refuelling, it seemed there were no vacancies available in the Royal Air Force and he began his Service career engaged in the maintenance of safety equipment, a broad category that included parachutes, dinghies of every shape and size, emergency kits and airborne lifeboats. After some time spent in these far from exotic pursuits, he talked his way into the presence of an engineer officer and more or less begged for a chance to get into the engineering side of the trade structure. Eventually he succeeded, and was allowed in with the promise that if he agreed to sign on for five years, he would be sent on an engineering course. As it happened, what with the cold war in Europe, the Berlin blockade and the hot war in Korea, the five years stretched eventually to eight.

After finishing his apprentice course he emerged as a fitter, airframe, and was posted to Kabrit, in Egypt, to work on that sturdy old warhorse, the Douglas Dakota. Kabrit was one of the bases on the south-western shore of the Great Bitter Lake, in an area to which the Royal Air Force had moved as part of the concentration that followed the withdrawal from the Nile delta in the years immediately after the war. As it contained no less than five transport squadrons — Nos 78, 114, 204, 215 and 216 — all equipped with Dakotas, he had plenty of material upon which to practise his technical skills. Initially, they had been lumped together in two large squadrons of twenty aircraft each, but this was an unmanageable arrangement for the conditions obtaining in 1947 and five smaller squadrons were created, forming a Transport Wing.

Subsequently Gerald was posted south to Shallufa, on the lower part of the canal north of Suez, working in the target-towing flight of Harvards and Beaufighters. Shallufa was actually the main bomber base for RAF Mediterranean and Middle East, its main function being to provide a secure base in the area should operations be contemplated against the Soviet Union. This was at the height of the cold war, which threatened to go hot at any moment, and the Berlin blockade had just started. Nevertheless, the prospect of Lancasters attacking Russia from Egypt in 1948 is a little difficult to visualise.

In fact, at about this time the bomber squadrons were withdrawn back to England into the bosom of Bomber Command; however, they, and the Lincolns that succeeded them, paid regular visits to Shallufa for deployment practice and for fighter affiliation training with the Tempests of 324 Wing based at Deversoir at the north end of Great Bitter Lake. The bomber deployment continued until 1949 under the code-name SUNRAY, and Gerald retains vivid memories of white-skinned Lancaster crews, clad in unfamiliar Bermuda shorts (surely the world's most ridiculous military costume) emerging from their aircraft to cries of 'Moon-men!' from the satisfactorily brown-kneed locals.

Shallufa was very much a desert outpost; most of the buildings were of wood and many of them were leaning over to one side. There was none of the spit and polish and parades that had characterised Kabrit. 'How charming', Gerald thought when he first saw it; 'What a delightful place!' It was very restful for the permanent staff. Actually it was considered such an uncivilised dump by the rest of the Command that a posting there practically guaranteed that you had been labelled

'undesirable'. It was certainly not fit for contact with the civilised bases to the north, where there were things like WAAFs; 'It was a rough place, it was'. But Gerald still remembers the Officer Commanding, Group Captain Canning; a most delightful man, who gave up one of the permanent concrete buildings for use by the Art Club.

After the Middle East Gerald had a home posting at West Malling in Kent, for service among the Meteors of No 500 (County of Kent) (Fighter) Squadron, Royal Auxiliary Air Force, and the delightful opportunity of some unofficial flying instruction in the Harvards and the two-seat Meteor 7s.

West Malling was an aerodrome of respectable (and civilian) antecedents: it had been a second-class landing ground called King's Hill in World War I and was taken over by the Royal Air Force in the 1930s, by which time it had grown up and become Maidstone Airport. It was the principal base for those squadrons engaging the 'doodlebugs' in 1944. No 500 Squadron moved in with their Meteor 3s when they reformed in Reserve Command in June 1946; by 1950 they were flying Meteor 4s and had transferred to Fighter Command.

No 500 Squadron was formed in 1931, but it was not until they received the Meteor (the first Auxiliary squadron so to do) that they became a fighter unit. Nos 500 to 504 Squadrons were formed originally as Special Reserve bomber squadrons, transferring to the Auxiliary Air Force during the expansion period. However, only 501 and 504 then became fighter units with the other Auxiliaries. They all vanished, with the rest of the Auxiliary squadrons, in the short-sighted and ill-advised surgery conducted on the RAF by their political masters in 1957. Incidentally, a very senior citizen of West Malling was still alive and well and flying at Old Warden, Bedfordshire, in 1990; owned in 1931 by Mr Lowe-Wilde of motor-glider fame from Kent Aeronautical Services, it was a Sopwith Dove, restored to become a Sopwith Pup by the Shuttleworth Trust. Not a lot of people know this.

Return to Civilian Existence

While Gerald was serving at West Malling, he paid a visit to the civic airport at Rochester, all-but-visible from the RAF station across the Medway valley; the aerodrome itself is hidden by the crest of Bluebell Hill on the North Downs, but the circuit traffic can be seen clearly on a decent day. Rochester town had been an early starter among the pioneers of civic airports, opening one in 1934; at the time of Gerald's visit it was still the site of Short Brothers' factory, where he might have seen his old desert friend the Beaufighter being reconditioned. There was also an active flying club, and here were based the Tiger Moths of Universal Flying Services, among others. Tiger Moths, as will be seen, were to play an important part in Gerald Coulson's life.

The object of the Rochester visit was to try and secure civilian employment in aviation when he left the Royal Air Force — a date that was now approaching fairly rapidly. When he went to see the chief engineer there with an account of his qualifications, he was met with enthusiastic approval. Gerald was, it seemed, just the sort of chap they were looking for and ought to be very useful; 'Come and see us as soon as you leave the Service'.

All this sounded very satisfactory, and after he had left the Royal Air Force and returned to a mundane civilian world he got in touch with them again. Absolutely nothing happened at all. He had been far too innocent to grasp the realities of such things as vacancies in the commercial world, and at the time of his application there were none available. So that was that.

The next stage was to go round to the local Labour Exchange in Chatham and see what they had to offer. What they had, in view of Gerald's experience as a Group 1 Engineer in the RAF, was a job testing and installing the systems in concrete mixers. All-hydraulic mixers were experimental at this time and there was a vacancy for someone with experience in hydraulics. It was Gerald's first introduction to your average vast assembly shop and he found the noise, apart from anything else, absolutely hellish. The job only lasted a short time; 'If this is civilian life', he thought, 'I'm going back into the Royal Air Force.' Looking back in 1990 to that particular episode, his only comment was: 'Well, it carved a notch on my staff of life.'

While contemplating his next move, he saw an advertisement in a newspaper calling for ex-Royal Air Force engineers to volunteer for service with the Royal New Zealand Air Force. He went round to New Zealand House in the Strand in London, volunteered as requested and was duly accepted by a Selection Board; he was given a six-year contract. However, to cover his options he had also written to British European Airways for employment, and to Hawker Aircraft Ltd at Dunsfold. When BEA wrote and offered him a job, he obviously felt a home posting was preferable and promptly accepted; he passed his entrance examination and was posted to the engineering base at Heathrow Airport, where BEA was just getting its first Viscounts. He was fortunate that the Royal New Zealand Air Force released him from his six-year contract without any fuss.

The Viscount was the world's first turbine-powered aircraft to operate passenger scheduled services, and the first British aircraft to sell in quantity in the United States of America. By a comfortable little coincidence Sir George Edwards, who was responsible for the design of the Viscount, became the patron of the Guild of Aviation Artists at its inception in 1971, and was still actively supporting the Guild from that position in 1990.

In 1950 British European Airways ran the world's first brief fare-paying schedules with turbines between London and Paris, and later another between London and Edinburgh for the Edinburgh Festival; the first sustained schedules, however, on the London-Rome-Athens-Nicosia route, began with the Discovery class Viscount 701s on 18 April 1953 — about the time that Gerald Coulson was joining the Corporation.

The Society of Aviation Artists

In 1954 there came a crucial turning point in Coulson's painting career. He read a letter in the aviation press, from a number of professional aviation painters, inviting interested artists to submit work. So he did submit to them some of his work in body colour, which was accepted. This was all enormously exciting, because it was the first time that he was actually able to meet all the big names in aviation painting, the founding fathers of the Society. They included Terence Cuneo, Roy Nockolds, David Shepherd, Michael Turner, Frank Wootton and John Young. Altogether there were about two dozen members.

By now, Gerald was deeply into his discovery of watercolours and body white and hog hair brushes.

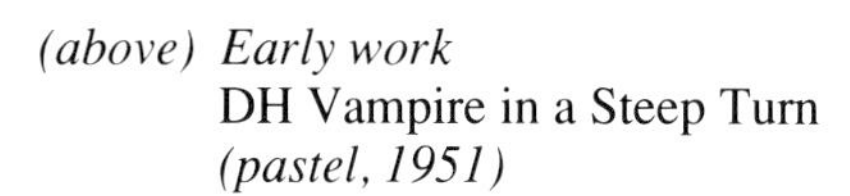

(above) Early work
DH Vampire in a Steep Turn
(pastel, 1951)

(below) A 1955 watercolour
Final Approach (as seen over the shoulder of the pilot of a DH Rapide)

Two watercolours produced for the 1955 Society of Aviation Artists' exhibition at the Guildhall in London

(above) 'Comet' Crew Carrying Out Checks Prior to Night Take Off

(below) Crew of 'Constellation' 749 Carrying Out Checks Prior to Taking Off

'. . . piling the results neat onto Whatman's NOT surface watercolour board with *dollops* of process white'. He was also discovering clouds and their overwhelming importance to his paintings. It was a period when exposure to the work of other artists and to public exhibition was particularly important, although he was obviously working on the right lines since his work was accepted and hung every year — and in his second year he was elected to membership, which at one fell swoop lifted him, as he said, 'into the same echelon as the others'. And of course it was here that he first met his ideal aviation artist, Frank Wootton.

In fact Gerald had already been lifted into the first echelon by Reyner Banham, writing in the June 1954 issue of the *Art News and Review* in a passage sufficiently rich and strange to warrant quoting *in extenso:*

. . . the experience of aviation is essentially dynamic, and the painter's art is static; the painter can depict with conviction every aspect of aviation except the one which matters — flight. The inaugural exhibition of the Society of Aviation Artists at the Guildhall Gallery, is full of conspicuous failures to recognise this fact, and a few, very few, heroic failures to surmount it when recognised — if one accepts the convention of paintings of aircraft in flight, one accepts a dead art.

In all probability it should not be judged as an aspect of art at all, and one should move over to the alternative convention of technical illustration. Here, in one sense, the heavy professionals — Cuneo, Coulson, Wootton, Nockolds — are outstanding, with their bold baroque compositions executed in a brash and convincingly vulgar style drawing on Munnings and R.O. Dunlop; and in another sense the stars of the 'cutaway view', admirably represented here by the elaborateness of Roy Cross and the dead-pan smoothness of Endsleigh Castle, are equally outstanding. But between these two peaks sags the slough of incompetence of aviation's Sunday painters, many of whom have yet to discover how to draw a doenut [sic] wheel in perspective, a slough in which incompetence is seldom relieved by the freshness of an unspoiled eye — except in a rare case like G.S. Speechley's stiff yet not incompetent study of the abstract Wellsian paraphernalia of Radar scanners.

Fortunately, not all critics felt about aviation art as did the remarkable Mr Banham and in 1955 Gerald's contribution to the exhibition was described as an 'exciting picture of the Super Mystère (No 80) tearing out of the sky and out of the canvas at the spectator', in an otherwise rather arid little review by Thurstan James in *The Aeroplane* of 23 September. In fact, looking through the reviews in the technical press of the paintings hung at Society exhibitions over the next few years, the same theme of speed and urgency in his paintings recurs.

'In a really vigorous watercolour . . . the best use of the dramatic quality of the open, thrusting nose and swept-back surfaces' — that was *Super Sabre Blast-Off* in 1956 (even the titles were heavily dramatic).

' . . . the forward movement of the take-off powerful and inevitable . . .': *Comet Departure* 1958.

Lightning Display in 1959 was recalled by R.E. Meddemmen in *Flight* as ' . . . a vast explosion of power as the machine hurtles out of the picture with the runway receding fast in a blur of speed'.

The Mystère is, in fact, the only watercolour from this period which survives for reproduction and is thus an important picture.

Of course these early paintings were not all dedicated to violent movement and foreshortening; there was a most intriguing composition at the Eighth Exhibition at the Guildhall in 1961. The Society of Aviation Painters had by this time merged its identity into the wider-based Industrial Painters Group, a move made to the members' own volition but one which did little to assist the future of the Society, for the Group itself had but a comparatively short career. Fortunately, as will be seen, a valid alternative was to present itself.

The painting for the exhibition was *Return to the Fold,* and portrays a P-51 taxying smartly out of the picture, framed by two interlocking rectangles that emphasise the movement to escape from the frame. All the drama, fury and energy inherent in a Coulson canvas of this period is concentrated, *not* in the movement of the aircraft, but in the picture-high figure of the urgently gesticulating marshaller, which drags the eye back into the right-hand side of the composition. Two distant Mustangs approaching head-on complete the complex geometry of the design. A second contribution, *First Across,* was not quite so successful; the Vickers Vimy up in the top right-hand section, pinned into the corner by the very high skyline, seems to have very little connection with the superb and convincing Atlantic waves.

As early as this in his career Coulson was signing his pictures quite deliberately on either the left or the right of the painting, after the manner of Wootton. But his reason is unique and revealing: he puts the name where it will best help to balance the composition. He confesses, too, that he sometimes signs paintings before they are actually finished as it seems to bring completion that little bit nearer.

While he was working at London Airport he had painted a picture of a British Overseas Airways Corporation Boeing Stratocruiser, at night on the North Side, and someone suggested that he should take it round to Samson Clarke, the advertising agency that was at that time handling BEA's advertising. So he did, and showed it to an amiable gentleman who admired it and pointed him in the general direction of the Central Art Agency. More than this, before Gerald left, he presented him with an original Frank Wootton sketch for a painting of a Douglas DC-4. It was painted in watercolour and body colour — a familiar combination — on two bits of watercolour paper glued one on top of the other to stiffen it up. However, when Gerald referred to it as a watercolour: 'Oh, no!', he was told. ' That's a gouache; *all* Woottons are gouaches.' Thus did Gerald Coulson discover gouache.

The Central Art Agency also received him kindly and gave him some work to do illustrating cars and aircraft. And all this time he was fully employed during each working day as a shift engineer, carrying out pre-departure checks on flights, on-the-spot rectifications, and general first-line servicing. Any painting that he managed to do had to be carried out painfully on hands and knees in his digs.

Another element in the development of Gerald Coulson's painting career now appears: in the 1950s there came into existence a remarkable gliding and light aircraft club called the Kronfeld Club. Robert Kronfeld was an Austrian gliding pioneer who more or less invented slope-soaring at the Wasserkuppe gliding site in Germany in about 1931. A few years later he came to England when life in Austria became politically impossible after the *anschluss.* He was killed not long after the war, test-flying a big tailless General Aircraft glider.

Many members of the club, which flourished in a basement in Eccleston Square, were amateur artists as well as pilots, and from 1958 they began to hold exhibitions of their work in the club — mostly paintings of sailplanes, as gliding enthusiasts dominated the place.

In 1964 the Kronfeld Club wrote to Coulson, inviting him, as a full member of the Industrial Painters Group, to join fellow group-member Roy Nockolds and Egerton Cooper to judge their annual exhibition; he was also invited to submit work. Both of these things he did, and also submitted a rich oil painting of a Slingsby Skylark 4 sailplane.

Roy Nockolds had been a Brooklands motor racing *aficionado* before the war and had made his reputation as an 'industrial' artist with his well known paintings of famous sporting and racing cars, veteran, vintage and modern; however, he was then less well known for his aviation paintings. In particular, he was intensely interested in sky and clouds. Egerton Cooper was principally familiar in aviation circles for a series of magnificent, richly painted pictures of airships (he worked with Lavery as a war artist in World War I), but was not otherwise an aviation artist. He showed a fine portrait of Barnes Wallis at the second Society of Aviation Artists Exhibition in 1955.

The Kronfeld Show was opened on 4 November by Bill Bedford, at that time chief test pilot at Dunsfold for Hawker Siddeley Aviation (for whom, indeed, if things had turned out differently, Coulson himself might have been working). At some stage in the judging proceedings Gerald was presumably told to go and wait outside, as his Skylark won first prize in the professional class — he would hardly have been privy to the decision. It had another claim to fame: in a catalogue where prices were extremely modest, many in single figures, it was priced at 80 guineas — second only to Egerton Cooper's contribution at 100 guineas.

Gerald continued to support the Kronfeld exhibitions; in 1966 the painters broke away from the Club and formed themselves into the Kronfeld Aviation Art Society, run by Hugo Trotter and Yvonne Bonham. Gerald was one of the founder members. In 1971 the name was changed to the Guild of Aviation Artists, something which coincided more or less with the demise of the Kronfeld Club. In 1990 Hugo Trotter and Yvonne Bonham were still with the Guild — Hugo as secretary and Yvonne as treasurer — and Coulson canvases still occasionally adorn the annual exhibitions.

One of Gerald's recollections from those early days of the Kronfeld concerns his first — and only — meeting with Peter Scott. This was at the 1964 exhibition when Scott, himself an active glider pilot as well as a painter, attended the opening. Naturally enough they talked painting, and he remembers receiving from the great man a remarkable piece of advice: 'What you must avoid is the happy accident.' 'Good Heavens!', thought Gerald, 'Without them I wouldn't be here.' Before all this excitement, however, while he was still with BEA, someone at the Engineering Base had shown Gerald an advertisement in the *News Chronicle* from a firm requiring 'A commercial artist for an aircraft design office'. This was quite patently something right up his street, so he applied for the job. The enquirer turned out to be Marshall of Cambridge, one of the more remarkable companies which has ever served the British aircraft industry, then and now — when, to be absolutely accurate, it is an aerospace industry.

Marshall of Cambridge (Engineering) Ltd began as automobile engineers in 1909; in 1929 they opened an aerodrome to house their newly formed Aircraft Division, transferring to the present one, Teversham, in the 1930s. Their considerable reputation was based on aircraft overhaul and repair: during the war they reconstituted Armstrong-Whitworth Whitleys and Albemarles, Hawker Typhoons and Douglas Dakotas; converted Mosquitos into radar-equipped night fighters, and operated a Civilian Repair Organisation for the Airspeed Oxford. There was also a thriving training operation employing Tiger Moths. After the war Marshall's undertook refurbishing and conversion work as well as military repair, dealing with Berlin Airlift Dakotas and later English Electric Canberras and many other types, including the Vickers Valiant. Maintenance and conversion work on civilian aircraft began to build up: there was a Gulfstream franchise and overhaul work on Bristol Britannias, as well as interior design and conversions for airlines, corporations and heads of state. In 1966 they worked on the Lockheed Hercules for the Royal Air Force (and converted one into the odd-looking and solitary W2 Weather-Herc at Farnborough). Alongside all this the flying club flourished and other light aircraft owners and organisations came and settled on the airfield. As a result of all this post-war activity, the drawing office and design office organisation had to be enlarged considerably, and it was in the course of that activity that Gerald Coulson was drawn into Marshall's orbit.

As a first step, he went round to the Central Art Agency and asked if he could borrow back some samples of the work that he had been doing for them, so he could make up a portfolio. Armed with these, he went up to Cambridge to see the company at its pleasant airfield on the Newmarket road. Shown into the technical publications section of the drawing office, he produced his samples, with which they were quite evidently very impressed, eventually admitting that they didn't have anyone there doing that sort of thing, but could he do technical illustrating, which was what they did need a lot of? Gerald promptly said 'Yes, of course', on the sound general principle of never saying 'No' to anything — without having any idea of the high quality of finished line work that would be required of him, as later he admitted. However, it turned out to be a very useful discipline that stood him in good stead afterwards.

In the event he was not only offered the job, but at a salary higher than that of the other technical illustrators in the office (some of whom may now be realising this for the first time); the beneficial result of his impressive case of samples. He went back to London by train and returned the originals to the agency, who immediately introduced the need for another decision by trying to persuade him that, rather than take on this very dubious new venture with Marshall, on work that was quite different from his present experience, he should come and work full time for them, for the same pay, where he could sit in the studio in London and paint cars and aircraft to his heart's content.

This was, of course, a great temptation and he worried for some time over the problem of which course to select for his future career. It would be very easy to stay in London, going on with work he knew he could cope with, but then he thought: 'If I go to Marshall's, I shall be acquiring a whole new series of skills and getting a salary into the bargain, and I can still find time to freelance for the agency as before.' So he went to Marshall's.

It really was totally new work, as far as he was concerned. In theory, he had been engaged on the basis of being already fully qualified and was being paid a very reasonable salary for so being, but in fact he was, initially at any rate, learning on the job, absorbing advice generously given by the people already working there and having to find out a great deal more for himself. He would be handed a great pile of engineering drawings and general arrangements which he had to sort out and inwardly digest, and from which he had to produce finished perspective work of very high quality. He found, however, that he had two things working for him: a very considerable knowledge of aircraft structures, and a good (in fact a lifelong) grounding in drawing them.

These advantages, and his natural abilities, paid off in the long run, for after eight years he had become head of the department, chief technical illustrator and — which was hardly surprising — company artist. In one capacity or another, he was responsible for producing the colour visuals of aircraft interiors for furnishing or refurnishing contracts, and designs for aircraft liveries. The designing and fitting out of aircraft interiors for executive or airline use had become, as already mentioned, one of the major parts of Marshall's business, and among the designs for which Gerald was responsible were those for the private aircraft of King Constantine of Greece and the Prime Minister of Nigeria, and for the airliners of Lloyd International, Aloha and Cambrian; the latter, it turned out, operating one of 'his' old BEA Viscounts (the one that is now part of the Imperial War Museum collection of civil airliners at Duxford, not very far from where Gerald now lives).

For the record, one part of the Cambrian livery he did not design was their Welsh dragon. This was passed over to him for incorporation in the livery by the founder and chairman of the airline, S. Kenneth Davies, who had produced it himself. Kenneth was a celebrated, extrovert Cardiff business man, *bon viveur,* private pilot (with an airstrip at his home in Ireland) and chairman of the Royal Aero Club. The said dragon, in a very sombre red, was repeated as a slightly depressing frieze round the bar in his London house; a bar where you were only allowed to drink White Ladies, which he mixed himself with great skill.

It was in his capacity as company artist that Gerald produced one of his dramatic, straight-off-the-runway-and-right-past-your-ear paintings of a British Overseas Airways Corporation VC-10 — one of the largest aircraft to pass through Marshall's hands — which formed the cover of a comprehensive brochure surveying all the company's activities.

Learning to Fly

At this point in the story, in 1959, another of Gerald Coulson's great interests crops up for the first time. He learnt to fly. There had been a continuous, or nearly continuous, tradition of club flying and light aircraft at Teversham since the pre-war occupancy of the Cambridge Aero Club before the war. When the latter's Gipsy Moths fled north to Prestwick at the outbreak of war, they were replaced by a great fleet of Tiger Moths, which until 1951 were used for training instructors for the Royal Air Force. 'Marshall's Messerschmitts', as they were known, were then replaced by de Havilland Chipmunks, but when civil flying was resumed after the war, the Cambridge Aero Club (run by Marshall) came home to roost, and operated their own silver Tiger Moths from the airfield.

In 1956, just before Gerald joined the firm, the Cambridge Private Flying Group was formed, operating their yellow and silver Tiger Moths from the old blister hangar down the perimeter track. On one of these, G-AOEI, Gerald went solo in 1960 (indeed, he qualified for his pilot's licence before he could legally drive a car!). He considered then, and still considers now, that he was extremely fortunate to have been taught by someone of the calibre of Bill Ison, the Chief Flying Instructor at the time. Bill Ison is still there as CFI in 1990, and both he and Gerald still fly G-AOEI.

It had always been Gerald's intention to learn to fly one day, but it was not until now, at Cambridge, that his determination met up with the second requirement — availability of aircraft. The third requirement, the money to pay for it, was another matter altogether. Flying with the Group at that time cost £2.65 (in post-1970 currency) and he could never afford more than thirty minutes at a time (in spite of which, his progress was remarkably rapid). Money was so tight, in fact, that he could not afford to throw away a landing and go round again (another five minutes' flying) something which, apart from anything else, certainly sharpened up his approaches.

In fact, he was sent solo after less than four hours' dual instruction; 'Of course, you've done a lot of gliding', they said. What the 'lot of gliding' actually amounted to was a couple of winch launches with the RAF at Biggin Hill, although in those days, that *was* quite a lot of gliding for some people.

Flying has always, since then, been an ongoing thing in Coulson's life and he has seized every available opportunity to build up flying hours and increase his experience, initially using all the usual channels open to impecunious private pilots, the commonest being parachutist-dropping and glider-towing. Of the former activity, he claims never to have understood the mentality of parachutists: 'Nothing would induce *me* to leave a serviceable aircraft!'.

Coulson in the cockpit of a D H Tiger Moth

By 1990 he had amassed a respectable 1,000 hours in his log book which includes flying a wide variety of vintage light aircraft as well as such exotic experiences as flying with the Red Arrows in a Hawk, and with Treble One Squadron in a Lightning — the latter, at Mach 1.52 at 36,000 feet, earning him membership of the 'Thousand Mile an Hour Club'.

Although his first, last and all-time flying love is the Tiger Moth, in the course of amassing his 1,000 hours or so 'in command', Gerald has flown a number of other aircraft, ranging from the tiny Dart Kitten and Turbulent to the Harvard — the latter being, in his considered opinion, 'quite docile and not as alarming as expected'. In between came a number of types ranging 'from the bland to the hairy'. In a *Which*-type survey he rated the Auster 6 glider tug as 'worst value for money' in most respects; for general handling and aerobatics the Chipmunk came well out on top. Among the rarer types in his log-book, the Proctor Kittywake was 'delightful', and the lumbering great Percival Prentice 'big' – which is probably as good an assessment as any. (Designed as a three-seat RAF trainer, one civil conversion claimed to seat seven.) At the hairy end was the Rollason Beta Formula One racer: 'It was five minutes ahead of me and I don't think I breathed out until I landed and the engine stopped.'

The Tiger Moth

Today the de Havilland Tiger Moth is to sporting aviation what the vintage Bentley is to sporting motoring: rare, desirable, difficult to drive well, and costly to purchase and to maintain. Unlike the 'spamcans' of current production — but like the Bentley — it also demands a warm, dry stable.

It was first introduced early in 1932 as the standard elementary trainer for the Royal Air Force, and served continuously until 1951, the last biplane in the Service. Derived from the basic and amiable Gipsy Moth, it was considerably rearranged in order to give instructors easier access to and exit from the front cockpit, thus saving time between sorties and allowing more rapid departure in an emergency — which was presumably considered more likely with a Service trainer than in a civil aircraft that the pilot had probably paid for himself and therefore had some interest in preserving.

Production of Tigers went on through World War II, many being built by non-aviation companies such as Austin Motors. Gerald's favourite, and the subject of *Sunday Morning,* was G-AOEI, built in 1939 and delivered to No 20 Maintenance Unit under its Service number, N6946, and then issued to No 81 Squadron. The latter had a curious history: it was scheduled to take Sopwith Triplanes to France in April 1917, but did not finally form until after the Armistice, after nineteen months of 'on-again, off-again' orders. It then became No 1 Squadron, Canadian Air Force, until it was disbanded in January 1920.

It reformed in France in 1939, out of the Air Component of the British Expeditionary Force Communications Squadron (probably just to shorten the name), with Tiger Moths and an even more unlikely mount, the Avro Rota autogiro. After the *débâcle,* N6946 was the only survivor to get back to Hendon with what was left of No 81 (Comm) Squadron — which must have been the only Royal Air Force squadron ever to be equipped with Tiger Moths. (They later converted to Hurricanes, went to sea in HMS *Argus* and fought in Russia.)

Our Tiger stayed at Hendon with the resident Communications Squadron, No 24, transferred to No 510 when it formed out of No 24 and saw out the war with them. It then spent five years in store, came out into use with Nos 12 and 5 Reserve Flying Schools, and spent the spring of 1953 at White Waltham (whence, in 1989, three other Tigers set out for the Soviet Union). After service there with the Home Command Maintenance and Service Unit it went back into store again, until it was sold to Flying Officer Freestone in 1955, one of the last Tigers to go; at this point it acquired its civilian identity. The Cambridge Flying Group bought it in 1958, after it had been rebuilt at Old Warden by the Shuttleworth Trust — since when this most remarkable of survivors has been immortalised in paint by the man who made his first solo in her.

The Tiger Moth, with all the subtleties involved in four wings with different sweep-back, dihedral and incidence, is even more difficult to portray satisfactorily than most biplanes, and few artists have in fact achieved this consistently. Coulson Tigers always look right, a legacy, no doubt, of his engineering training and of his great personal familiarity with the breed (fully one third of his total flying hours have been logged in Tigers). The only other really competent biplane draughtsmen that come immediately to mind are Leonard Bridgman who was also an engineer by training, and Michael Turner, John Young and Charles Thomson, all of whom had the same rigorous commercial training on mechanical subjects that Gerald underwent, also in commercial studios. In addition Michael Turner served in the Royal Electrical and Mechanical Engineers, but he doesn't think that helped.

Career Breaks

While Gerald was working for Marshall's, learning to fly and freelancing for the Central Art Agency, the latter asked him to come and see them to discuss a very important commission. A new, very high speed research aircraft, the Bristol 188, was being built at Filton. It was nowhere near complete, but de Havilland, who were providing the engines, wanted a painting of it for an advertisement on the front cover of an impending issue of *The Aeroplane* (it appeared on the issue for 10 October 1960).

There was no particular problem in producing the background information for the painting; he was given lots of photographs of a model of the complete aircraft, and he was invited to go down to Filton to sketch the (very) incomplete airframe. He duly travelled down there by train to make his sketches, and one of the details of the journey that he still remembers was the comfortable — and novel — sensation of being collected from Temple Meads railway station in a chauffeur-driven company Austin Princess. One of the very big ones; the 'Vanden Plas mini' version of the Princess had not yet appeared.

The job, to quote Coulson himself, 'was a bastard'. But it was a very important one and he knew that he was perfectly capable of handling it. Incidentally, it was his normal practice, while a client was talking to him, to be turning the subject over in his mind and mentally composing the picture, so that by the time they had finished talking, he knew just what he was going to paint and exactly how he was going to set about it. One cannot help wondering how the customer reacted to the inevitably rather abstracted look that must have accompanied this process; many must have thought, with Dickens' celebrated Dr Blimber in *Dombey and Son,* that they had not succeeded in securing his attention. However, in the case of the 188, there *was* a very large and quite unexpected snag. They wanted it in oils.

Why? It appeared that the de Havilland Engine Company, who had commissioned it, wanted the original to hang in their Board Room and wanted it to be in oils on canvas. Canvas. He brooded on this all the way back to London on the train.

As an initial gesture, he went out and bought a large stretched canvas. It measured thirty inches by forty and looked to his troubled eye like a young cinema screen. He also bought a brand new easel — which he still has, twenty-nine years later — and a whole lot of tubes of oil paint. He deliberately purchased the same colours that he was accustomed to using in gouache and watercolour, knowing that he could get the same results and that he would at least feel at home with a familiar palette.

With a bottle of turps replacing the usual water jar, and, for lack of any alternative way of approaching the problem, he employed exactly the same technique as he used in the other medium — and it worked beautifully. So beautifully, in fact, that afterwards he abandoned his heavy watercolours and his gouache and got into oils in the biggest possible way. And from that day he has never looked back.

The next turning point in his career as a painter came from Heffer's, the people whom he used to

employ when he had any framing to be done. There was a man in the artists' materials department who suggested that Gerald should take some of his originals and have fine art prints made out of them. This was a novel and interesting suggestion. Gerald was familiar, of course, with fine art prints, usually by Vernon Ward or Peter Scott. One looked at them, admired them, and that was that. It had never occurred to him that he might himself join this august band, that paintings of his might aspire to become fine art prints. But after all, when you got down to it, someone was going to do it. Why should it not be he?

The gentleman at Heffer's suggested he get in touch with Frost and Reed of Bristol who were the biggest print people in the business, and handled clients like Frank Wootton, Montague Dawson and Russell Flint. So he photographed half a dozen of his landscapes (including no aviation work at this stage) and sent them off to Frost and Reed. They wrote back to him and asked if they might have a look at the original paintings, which was an encouraging sign.

He had been asked to send the originals down. He decided, however, that this would take far too long and he could not bear to hang about waiting for the verdict, so in the end he caught the milk train down to Bristol and carried the paintings up to Frost and Reed himself. When he entered the gallery it was a memorable moment, finding himself, a new boy, literally among the experts: 'There were these *original* Russell Flints and Montague Dawsons on the floor, leaning against the wall. I picked up a Russell Flint original, just like that, quite casually.'

Amongst the landscapes he had brought with him was a painting of a showman's steam traction engine, *The Iron Lady* (see p37); when the originals had all been inspected the gallery people said: 'We are not interested in any of the others, but would you let us publish this traction engine? If we publish *that* it will make you world-famous.' A startling statement for a young man still rather out of his depth and a bit overawed by Russell Flint and Montague Dawson.

They gave him £75 for the original and the copyright, but no royalties. Coulson was thrilled to bits. After all, in 1960 that was a whole month's salary. No royalties seemed rather hard, but as he said afterwards: 'In the mood I was in, I would have given it to them for nothing.' In fact *The Iron Lady* did extremely well as a print, and was still selling in 1990.

That traction engine was his introduction to the world of the Fine Art Society. Frost and Reed came back to him in 1966 and wanted another painting for a print. Could he paint a railway engine? Of course he could paint a railway engine. Which one would they like? With their Bristol affiliations, it would naturally be a Great Western Railway locomotive and they settled on the King Class locomotive *King Richard I*. Thirty of these superb 4-6-0 passenger locomotives were built between 1927 and 1930, *King Richard I* being one of the last to leave the shops. They stayed in first class service for almost thirty years, right up to the end of steam with British Rail post-war. In BR hands draughting was modified to take account of the much inferior coal then available, and towards the end of their careers twin blast pipes and double chimneys were fitted to improve performance. Apart from that the original design was unchanged. The locomotive is shown at its usual pre-war trade, hauling the Cornish Riviera Express on a section of what the company referred to as the 'holiday line'.

In 1935, to celebrate their centenary, the company introduced special rolling stock on this line, calling the train *The Centenary Riviera*. Because of the more spacious proportions of the main line Great Western loading gauge, a relic of their broad gauge origins, the stock could be made much wider and more comfortable than that of other companies, although it was banned from certain routes because of its width. Traffic on the route was exceptionally heavy and the Cornish Riviera Express was the flagship train of the Great Western Railway — who kept their name longer than any other railway in British history; from 1835 until nationalisation in 1948.

Great Western Express, as the print was titled (see p36), delighted Frost and Reed and they proposed to follow up their success with their new artist by moving into another of his specialist subjects. Could he paint them an aeroplane? Certainly he could paint them an aeroplane. For obvious reasons it had better be a Bristol aeroplane, and so he painted them his Bristol Bulldog (p38).

It was deservedly a most popular print, selling well over several years; like the railway locomotive that preceded it by a year, it cost £2 7s 6d (£2.23) including purchase tax (a sort of naive native predecessor to VAT). In this print, the artist's growing preoccupation with clouds and aerial perspective is clearly to be seen.

The subject of this portrait is K2184, one of a second batch of a hundred Bulldog Mk IIAs delivered between June 1931 and February 1932, and taken on strength by No 41 Squadron. In 1990, the Squadron, one of the last two units still equipped with the Anglo-French Jaguar, were special guests of the Guild of Aviation Artists at the opening of their Annual Open Exhibition. The Bulldog Mk IIA was fitted with the more powerful Bristol Jupiter VIIF engine of 440hp and was a real gentleman's fighting carriage, much beloved by the many pilots who flew it. At the height of its service career in 1932, it equipped ten of the thirteen fighter squadrons of the Royal Air Force forming the air defence of Great Britain. With its yellow 'B' Flight wheel discs, K2184 is the very epitome of the latest Service fighter of its day: radio-equipped, with navigation lights and underwing brackets for Holt landing flares for night as well as day fighting, it has a generator on the lower wing to supply electrical power and a camera gun above the centre section to record the simulated performance of the twin Vickers guns that were its standard armament.

Royal Air Force Bulldogs were all scrapped before World War II (this one being struck off charge on 4 July 1938), although some Finnish Mk IVs saw action in the Winter War against the Soviet Union.

The gallery then requested another aircraft painting to make a pair with the Bulldog, and Gerald chose the Hawker Fury as a suitable stablemate — partly because it happened to be the first one that came to mind and partly because he thought it a supremely beautiful aircraft (p39).

He was still working for Marshall, at his drawing board in the drawing office, when this series of prints for Frost and Reed was begun, and as well as the problems of working under far from ideal conditions in his digs to produce the paintings, he was finding that having to paint from photographs — in the case of the historic aircraft — made things very difficult. So when his telephone rang in the office one morning and Frost and Reed told him that *Great Western Express* had come sixth in the Fine Art Guild's Top Ten, he resigned on the spot on the strength of the news — and has never looked back.

When he contemplates this early period as a full-time freelance artist, he still finds it slightly unreal. After all, as he says, he could very easily just have sat around for the first three years and frightened himself to death, instead of commanding the great success that he did — he had to generate a continuous flow of work in order simply to survive. The main problem, however, was not getting the work; he has never had a picture that did not sell. The problem was getting paid; often it was '. . . a hell of a job to get the money', and isolated cases of non-payment do still occur.

He has, in fact, only two of his own originals in his possession, both executed as exercises: one is a study of water lilies in a fishpond in a house he once rented not far from his present home; the other is a portrait of a horse, an exercise in the effect of light on a highly polished animal. This particular horse was called Sweet Reclaim, and was produced for him by the stables after he had casually enquired of someone in a pub in Newmarket if he had a pretty horse he could paint.

While he is adamant that he would never want to earn a living in any other way, he has to admit that creating paintings for a livelihood is a pretty exhausting affair. After two to three hours of solid painting, with every last half inch of the surface having to harmonise with the whole, it becomes a constant battle between him and the canvas. He also finds that at a certain stage, just to complicate matters, it becomes impossible to stop.

After many years of painting, it may be assumed that one's technique at least must have reached an adequate technical level (and he feels that there are no problems in that direction), but not everything one paints is a commission and there is the constant strain of being always under the compulsion to produce new and exciting pictures for the people who go about asking each other, 'What's Coulson coming up with next?' The trouble is, of course, that they don't actually know what they want until they have seen it. A real chicken-and-egg situation. This constant effort to be new and original and exciting every single time can be very wearing.

There is, too, an enduring misconception about which he feels very strongly indeed:

> Of any other professional, people say, 'Oh, he must have worked terribly hard to get where he is now'. But if you are a painter, they say 'Oh well, after all, it's a gift'. Well, it's very definitely not a gift; it's *very, VERY* hard work. The gift is the capacity to press on continually, and to work hard *even* when it is all going wrong.

There is no short cut to acquiring technique. Technique is practice over the long years, it is trial and error, it is using the eyes God gave you to observe the fall of light, the turn of a surface, and so on. As to what Gerald thinks is important in a picture; well, as Stacey Marks once told him in his gallery: 'If a thing looks painted, it's no good', adding 'the two most important ingredients in any picture are the beauty of the subject and the skill of the artist.' With both of these statements Gerald Coulson agrees — and on his own account adds draughtsmanship firmly to the list; which is hardly surprising, when you consider his training in that particular subject. But still, for him, in common with a large number of other painters, the one great fundamentally important thing in any picture is light.

He was also discovering, as already noted, another great and beautiful truth about painting. For years he had looked at skies simply as a place for his aeroplanes to sit — but suddenly realised that if you took away the aeroplane, you had a landscape. (This view, it must be admitted, is the direct opposite of the approach of more than one member of the Guild of Aviation Artists, who are not above adding an aeroplane to a landscape to render it eligible for a Guild exhibition.)

In fact, the landscape painters of the turn of the century have had a great influence on Coulson's work; in particular, he admires the paintings of Henry Bright, Sidney Percy, Benjamin Leader and Sir Alfred Munnings.

There were six prints issued by Frost and Reed altogether; the last two were *Lone Spitfire* (I) (p37), the penultimate print and the first of a long line of successful Spitfire paintings; and finally *Black Label Bentley* (p37) which became runner-up in the Fine Arts Guild Top Ten.

Black Label Bentley

One does not think of Gerald Coulson primarily as a painter of cars, but if he was going to paint a car it would have to be this one; the 4½ litre Bentley. About as elegant as a Shire horse but with a good deal of that massive animal's dignity, and just as hairy a set of heels, the Bentley is unique among sporting cars. Peter Hull and Nigel Arnold-Foster, in their delightful joint work *A Vintage Car Casebook*, have this to say concerning its origins: 'The Bentley motor car was the motor car made by W.O. Bentley

. . . the car was W.O.'s and no one else's . . . truly the extension of one man's personality.' They go on to point out that in his youth, W.O. was fascinated by the larger railway engines of the late nineteenth century and served his apprenticeship at the locomotive works at Doncaster. Which, as they say, figures.

The original Bentley was the 3 litre, and delightful in every way; the 4½ which followed in 1927 was, by comparison, a bit of a monster (both are described in the *Casebook* as 'brutish and noisy'), but it won in competition and was generally rather larger than life. It was H.R.S. 'Tim' Birkin who inspired the 'blower' Bentley 4½, with an elegant Amherst-Villiers supercharger in the nose providing about eight lb of boost, for competition at le Mans. Birkin and Dorothy Paget ran a team of five competition cars and another fifty were built as production cars, the minimum run needed to qualify for the '*Vingt-quatre heures du Mans*', which was, of course — and still is — an event for production motor cars.

Bentley himself never liked the blower but the blown 4½ became a highly popular mount, and enjoys unique vintage status in modern hands, even if its performance might make it, to go back to the *Casebook*, 'the delight of the oil sheiks and the despair of the conservationists'. Bentleys were first and fifth in the 1928 le Mans, and second, third and fourth in 1929. Bigger cars followed — 6, 6½ and 8 litre models — but Bentley finances were always 'a little tight under the arms', as Tony Harding has it, and in 1931 they were bought out by Rolls-Royce.

The car that Coulson painted bids fair to be one of the most historic Bentleys of all time. One of the five Birkin team cars, it raced in the Tourist Trophy and at le Mans in 1929, and in the Double Twelve event, the Irish Grand Prix and the TT in 1930. It was the car used to advertise the production blown 4½ in *The Autocar*, and in 1990 was still alive and well, living with Mr George Daniels in the Isle of Man.

That business of different coloured labels to denote the various marks of Bentley, incidentally, was never approved or used by the firm and has led to a certain amount of confusion. Just for the record, the theory was that you got a blue label on the standard 3 litre, red on the 3 litre Speed model, and green on the '100mph' version; black on the 4½ blue again on the standard 6½ and green on the 'Speed Six'. The 8 litre and the despised 4 litre had dark blue labels. But as you could get any colour label you liked put on your car by the works — who ignored the whole system anyway — it gets a bit academic round the edges.

The car has been painted standing outside the gates of St John's College, Cambridge, for no particular reason except that this fitted the publisher's request for a dignified setting. Gerald's only comment on this was that there turned out to be as much work in the gates as in the car.

Lone Spitfire (I) (p37) represents, to some extent, the end of one period in Gerald Coulson's 'printing history'. However, it could also be regarded as the painting which marks the beginning of a very important and continuing facet of his career, because it initiated his obsession with this beautiful aircraft which, with his increasing mastery of the painting of sky and cloud, combined to make his ever-growing line of Spitfire portraits among the most popular in his entire output. The Spitfire print crystallised the particular appeal of his work to the public; a long way now from any element of 'bold, baroque . . . brashness', his paintings provide the realism demanded by the enthusiast and the evocation of nostalgia demanded by the subject. A commonsense approach to the whole treatment of the composition prevents the sentiment ever slipping over into sentimentality. A great part of this success, without doubt, must lie in his practical approach to his subject; his eye is the eye of a trained engineer and of a man accustomed to absolute technical fidelity to a design in his drawing. Indeed, given his talent as a painter, it would be impossible for his intense admiration for, and delight in, good aircraft design and engineering not to shine through his work. Which boils down, really, to a variation on an old aphorism: 'If it's built right, you should paint it right.'

This particular Spitfire, DW-K, is a Mk Ia of No 610 (County of Chester) Squadron, Royal Auxiliary Air Force, a unit which, like all the Auxiliaries, distinguished itself profoundly during the Battle of Britain and throughout the rest of the war. Up to the beginning of 1939, the squadron was a light bomber unit like the other Auxiliaries, but transferred, as they all did, to Fighter Command; it narrowly escaped being issued with the abominable Defiant, receiving Hurricanes instead at the beginning of September, and then swapping them for Spitfires at the end of the month.

Posted south from Prestwick in time to plunge into the maelstrom of fighting over Dunkirk, the squadron

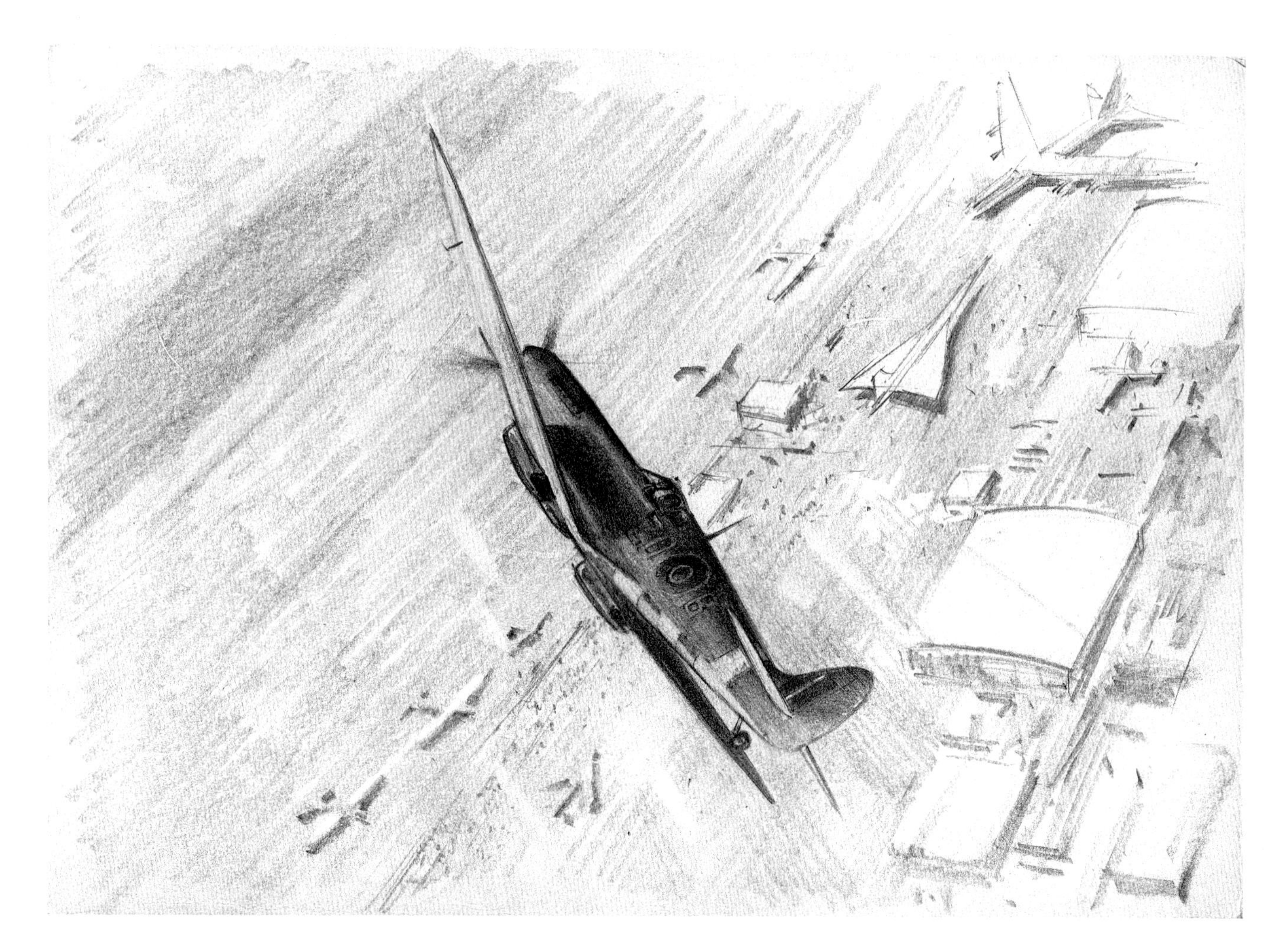

went on to cover itself in glory in the Battle of Britain, fighting out of Biggin Hill or Gravesend until the end of August, when it was withdrawn to Acklington for a much needed rest.

The painting itself presents few complexities or curiosities of design, apart from the fact that the artist has chosen to position his subject in the one place one was always taught *not* to position it — bang in the middle. (Of Coulson on the subject of what one is taught and not taught, in that context, more anon.) Its success seems to stem from the dominating part played by the dramatic, back-lit cloud formations, pinned at the bottom of the picture by a subdued east coast landscape with a subtly suggested horizon-line implicit among the shadows of the cloud bases. The aircraft itself, in this *milieu,* draws the eye back to the centre of the picture very successfully. Gerald himself would undoubtedly agree that this vindicates his very positive views on the subject of art training.

Widening Recognition

Gerald was immensely proud of those first six prints; very pleased, as a new boy, to have made it into the top ten, and beginning to realise that in consequence he was now 'in with a chance'. Indeed, at this time he began selling work to a number of other galleries; he was approached by Robinson's Calendars and Diaries, who had started a publishing company called Bristol Galleries, and eventually did quite a lot of work for them. The Alexander Gallery in Bristol also took work from him, and so did Stacey Marks in Eastbourne.

Most of the paintings he did for the Bristol Gallery were landscapes. This aspect of his work really began when he discovered, after painting the Bristol 188, that he really could handle oils; he had created no landscapes as such in his gouache days, although even at that stage he had begun to create landscape backgrounds — employing some 60 to 70 per cent sky — because they were required for his aircraft paintings. Landscapes, he claims, were 'a doddle' compared to aircraft; all you had to do to get one was not paint the aircraft. It was simple. He continued to paint landscapes — most of which were imaginary ones rather than records of one particular place — having realised, when he took the momentous decision to give up his job and paint for a living, that he could not possibly survive on commissions for aircraft paintings alone. He had already begun to take a great interest in the English landscape painters of around the turn of the century and after leaving the office, with nothing else to do, turned out paintings one after the other, discovering the simple but beautiful fact that the more you painted, the better you got and the better you got, the more you sold.

The United States of America now intruded upon Gerald's life: he was approached by a dealer who sold original English paintings in the States — he would spend six months of every year in the United Kingdom buying pictures, and then ship them across to America and tour with them for the rest of the year, selling to other dealers. He now wanted to include Gerald among his regular suppliers of genuine original English paintings. When the deal was finally settled with this gentleman, the arrangement proved to work very well, as it enabled Gerald to accumulate pictures, take them all down to Bristol and deliver them, and then go back home to start on the next load.

It was during this period that he heard about an African Wildlife Show that was to take place at Reno, Nevada, to raise funds for that cause. He was asked if he would contribute nine paintings for the occasion, which would be auctioned and the proceeds from one of them donated to the Wild Life Fund. Nine months of intensely hard work produced the paintings, but in the event the whole exercise turned into a disaster area because he had to expend a great deal of time and energy before he eventually managed to get the money due to him. All of which was rather depressing.

Some good, however, did emerge from all this disappointment. The Reno Gallery had asked him for a photograph of himself at his easel to illustrate an article about the exhibition. The photograph, when published, was seen by the proprietors of the Pace Gallery in Houston, which had already had considerable success with English landscapes bought from the first American dealer with whom Gerald had been involved.

Although the gallery owner, Charles Pace, had had several Coulsons through his hands, including the one of which Gerald was working in the photograph, he knew nothing about the artist; it now occurred to him to try and contact Gerald with a view to dealing with him direct.

The article contained no clue as to how the artist might be contacted, but did mention that he undertook glider towing for the Cambridge University Gliding Club. Armed with this meagre information, Charles Pace contacted a friend in England, a solicitor in Stockport, to whom, with that touching faith in the essential helpfulness of individuals that is common among North Americans and Australians but sadly not elsewhere, he simply sent the cutting from the magazine and the terse instruction, 'Find this man'.

The Stockport solicitor sensibly wrote to the Cam-

bridge University Gliding Club enclosing a letter to Gerald. This was handed to Gerald at home on Friday evening, by the club's chief flying instructor. It invited him to communicate with a solicitor in Stockport, 'when he might hear something to his advantage'. True to type, his correspondent failed to state what that something actually was, and Gerald spent a happy weekend dreaming of fortunes from long-lost relatives, or the possibility of inheriting a title. The whole thing was cleared up satisfactorily on Monday, and later he found himself shipping six canvases to the Pace Gallery, Houston (in Texas).

Charles Pace took more work from him, and after this in May 1976 organised a week-long one-man show in Houston for him. It was a great success, and was followed by a similar and equally successful one in Dallas (everyone knows where Dallas is!).

He supplied the Pace Gallery with work for some time, but work in Britain was meanwhile building up and things had got to the stage where it was considerably easier to satisfy the home market as his first priority (largely because answering the American demand also created considerable packaging and shipping problems), so that he gradually pulled out of America. He never divorced himself from it entirely, however, and quite a lot of his work eventually came to rest in the United States. Most of this was English landscape, but as a result of the Dallas and Houston one-man shows, there were a number of commissions for paintings, mostly from ex-aircrew, of B-17s and other wartime aircraft.

Some Reflections on Artistic Achievement

Looking at the broader aspects of Gerald Coulson's work, his recipe for success is brief and very simple; talking to him, one is left in no doubt whatsoever about his views on painting and about how he orders

his priorities. To clarify and apply these aims has been a long struggle, involving many years of painfully gathered experience, the consolidation of successful techniques and the development of his own natural skills of handling paint and composition. And at the end, it is distilled into those two cardinal precepts of his art: light and the skill of the painter.

Light is the key word; light, shining out of the canvas, sometimes the full, broad light of day, but often — far more often — the diffused light of the twilight zones, the light of a masked sun reflecting off cloud, water and foliage. He does no underpainting, so the clarity of the brilliantly handled areas of colour is not dimmed, and these rely for much of their effect upon the white canvas thrusting light up to the surface of the picture. His sensitivity to light conditions is reflected by the treatment of the broad daylight canvases such as *Hay Loading* and *Gathering Storm* compared with the dawn or late evening scenes. There is a rich impasto to the first two, a recognition of the stronger quality of the light which is especially evident in the treatment of the gathering storm clouds, and this contrasts strongly with the delicate, transparent areas of colour in the other paintings.

Coulson has a natural affinity with the grey mists of early morning: they spread seductively across the background of his paintings, softening outlines, creating steep aerial perspective and flattening the gradations of distance into one or two vertical planes like sublimated stage scenery; planes in which the individual details of trees, hedges and hills fall back into almost abstract shapes. At the other end of the day are the equally powerful, carefully designed and carefully controlled, back-lit landscapes bathed in the rich glow or afterglow of late evening.

An almost universal characteristic of these landscapes, in their design and in their execution, is the simplicity and tranquillity that is so much a key to Coulson's emotional and structural approach to each. A very frequent characteristic too, is the domination of the land by the sky, partly, one feels, from his aviation experience, and partly, no doubt, from the very nature of the flat East Anglian scene in which he has spent much of his working life.

Virtually none of Coulson's landscapes are actual reproductions of a natural scene. He does not by any means believe that nature necessarily gets it right every time: *au contraire,* you cannot rely on nature; you can, indeed you often must, rearrange her to obtain the reactions you want from the spectator. What he *does* believe very strongly is that an artist's success in getting results lies in the proper use of his own developed skills; that *the artist* must ensure that what he has created inside that particular frame, what he has done and designed, is pleasing and exciting; and he adds, characteristically — it must make people look at it and wonder how it was done. In pursuit of these aims, in both detail and grand design, Coulson canvases are built up from detail observed, recorded or remembered from any number of previous experiences and any number of sources.

It is not the least part of Coulson's skill, and his success as a landscape painter, that he can bring such intensity of feeling and thoroughness of design into the use of what one might reasonably call the stock elements of composition. In his hands the man walking his dog, the fisherman, the carts and the patient horses, the stag and the village church declare an originality from which a lesser mortal must fall short. Nothing, even the stag, that most flamboyant of show-offs, is allowed to escape the destiny to which Gerald has assigned it, or to become a random entry into the design: for Coulson, there are no random entries.

If there is no doubt about his positive creed, there is equally no doubt about what he dislikes, and there are certain subjects upon which he can be surprisingly vocal: surprisingly, because Gerald is a man whom one would ordinarily regard as being, like Professor Higgins of *My Fair Lady,* 'a most *forgiving* man'.

On the subject of art schools and formal art training — of which, it will be recalled, he was entirely innocent himself — Coulson is adamant. All art schools are a waste of time. They stifle initiative and inculcate outworn and obsolete notions of painting, and since (as far as he can see)most art students eventually become art teachers, this only serves to perpetuate the errors. At the time, he felt that the schools should all be closed down and the money given to nurses or any other equally deserving cause. This would appear to have some affinity with the classic opinion of many graduates of art schools that 'Those who can, paint; those who can't paint, teach; and those who can't teach, criticise'.

As for the last category, the critic and art expert, his stance is simplicity itself: 'Who are all these people and where do they come from? And who makes up their dreadful jargon?'

As far as art experts are concerned, he might well agree with the gentleman from the Royal Aerospace Establishment at Farnborough that the word 'expert' comes from 'x', an unknown quantity, and 'spurt', a drip under pressure.

Gerald Coulson has always claimed to have absolutely no business acumen (a common attitude among artists, one might add). In support of this claim he cites an interview with his bank manager at the start of his career. The latter admitted that he had never had an artist as a client before, but he was sufficiently intrigued, on acquiring one, to ask to see some of Gerald's work. In the course of the subsequent conversation on an artist's life and hard times, he learned that an art dealer could take an artist's work away and display it to the public without making any compensatory financial arrangement with him. He was absolutely horrified. Here were men being supplied with a free exhibition at absolutely no risk to themselves. What was more, they delayed payment on work sold for as long as possible. The moral justification of this appeared to him to be dubious; after all, if the dealer were to buy a picture at auction, which he frequently did, he would certainly not be allowed to carry it away without paying for it first.

It was, occasionally, difficult to recover Mr Coulson's attention from these 'outrageous, preposterous wrongs' and realign it upon the normally even tenor of his career. Not that he is alone in this characteristic; conversations with David Shepherd tend to take an equally exuberant turn.

To return to the next development in Gerald's career, in 1978 he submitted three subjects to Solomon and Whitehead: *The Ploughman and the Sea* (p46), *Winter Sunlight* (p34) and *Outbound Lancaster* (p48). (At that time, his output of aeronautical subjects was around 10 per cent of the total. Subsequently, interest in the aviation prints has ensured that the percentage continues to rise.)

Solomon and Whitehead were so impressed with the paintings that they were moved to comment that their selection committee had never seen work of such a standard before. All three, as prints, made the top ten: *The Ploughman and the Sea* at number one, *Outbound*

Lancaster at number three and *Winter Sunlight* at number six. Sales continued to go up, and all three were still selling well in 1990, twelve years later. From this start of Coulson's association with Solomon and Whitehead, sales have continued steadily to increase with *Quiet Forest,* as already mentioned, passing the half-million mark.

The increasing demand for paintings for prints leaves Coulson with little time to undertake private commissions; exposure from the publishers gives him all the work he can conveniently handle. Occasionally they will ask him to tackle a specific subject, but usually the choice is left to him. In addition, the very popular limited editions are now generating more work, on both sides of the Atlantic. Another result of this preoccupation with fine art prints and commissions is that Gerald has had very few one-man shows; indeed, in England, no more than two. Both took place in the Halcyon Gallery in Birmingham. The gallery had been started by a young man who had failed a course at the Royal Agricultural College outside Cirencester (a feat generally regarded as being impossible) and had made the Halcyon one of the most prestigious venues in Britain, its successes including David Shepherd's first exhibition outside London.

The first Coulson one-man show took place there in 1986; the second in 1988. In between, he took part in an exhibition, with other artists, to mark the rebuilding and refurbishing of the gallery in 1987. Following his initial experience in the fine art world, it must have been a source of some satisfaction to Gerald that one of the others represented was Sir William Russell Flint. In 1988 the Halcyon displayed fifty of his works, the largest collection of them yet seen in one place, along with signed limited edition prints and fine art prints. The advertisements in the daily press for this unique feast, which included both aviation and landscape paintings, described him as 'Britain's most distinguished landscape and aviation artist'.

Shortly before this event he had contributed significantly to the funds of the Imperial War Museum at Duxford, a quiet village in Cambridgeshire some two miles from his studio, by presenting them with two paintings for auction.

Now used by the Imperial War Museum, and base for various beautifully restored World War II aircraft (many of which are still flown), the historic ex-RAF fighter airfield at Duxford not only provides Gerald with a wealth of reference material for subject matter, but also gives him the opportunity to indulge in his favourite pastime of flying the several aircraft at his disposal, at the drop of a brush.

Looking back to the start of his career as a painter, and into the future, Gerald comments:

In 1969 I took my chance in what I now know to be a tough, demanding and precarious profession. Through the eventual happy association with the Fine Art publishing trade my work has enjoyed worldwide exposure and presented me with the privilege and opportunities to meet distinguished and interesting personalities, as well as opening doors for extensive travel. At times it can be quite lonely — but always exciting. No two tasks are ever the same and one never knows what is just around the corner.

The evolution of each new subject on a canvas quite frequently leads to the discovery of a new formula for acquiring desired effects. Keeping these precious prizes always in mind develops the technique and contributes to the steady and certain improvement of one's painting and confidence.

There is always room for improvement.

PRELIMINARY SKETCHES

Thunder and Lightnings *(p67)*

A Pilot's View *(p91)*

Thunder in the Hills *(p72)*

See p57

See p57

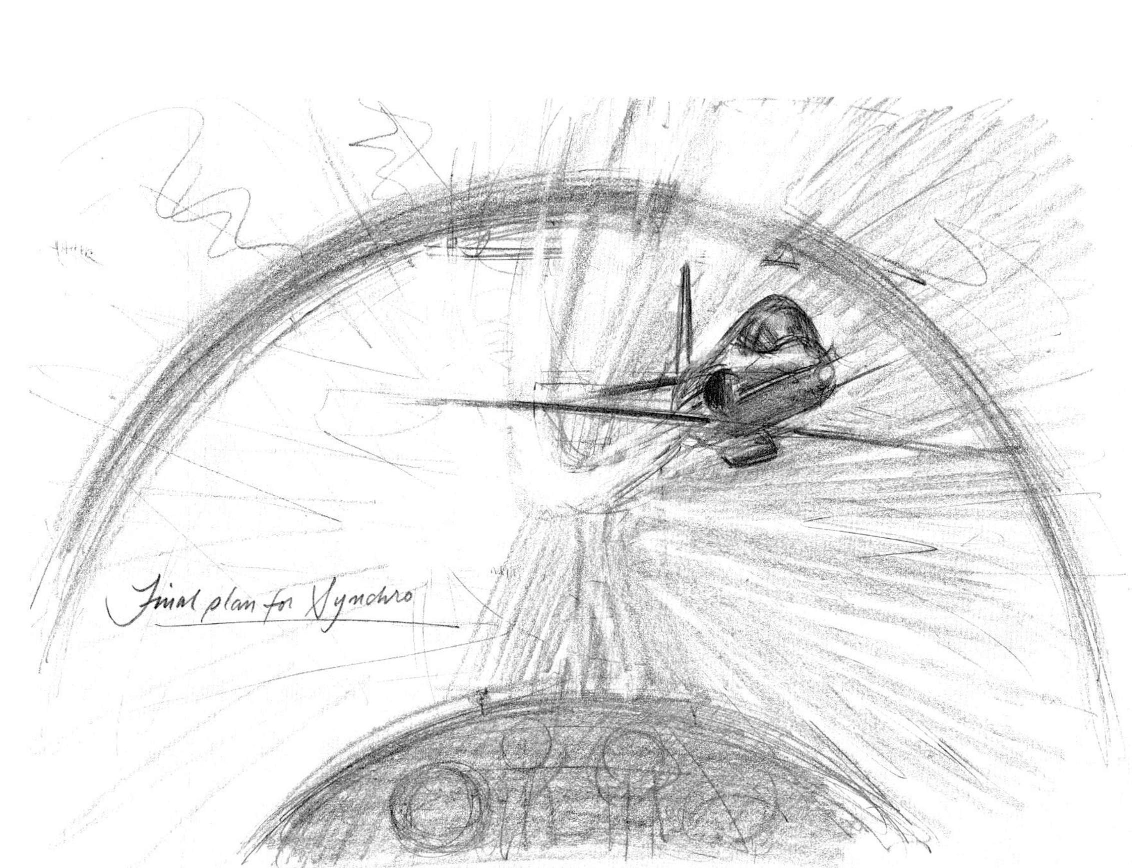

Synchro *(p68)*

See p69

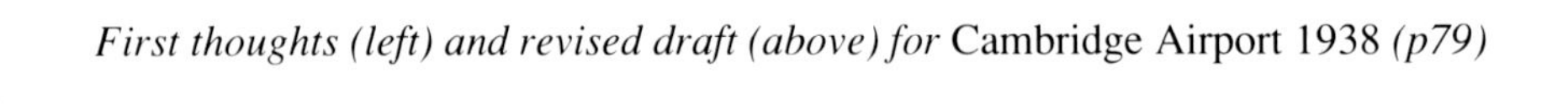

First thoughts (left) and revised draft (above) for Cambridge Airport 1938 *(p79)*

The Plates

See p95

SUNDAY MORNING

de Havilland DH. 82a 'Tiger Moth,' G-AOE1

"my favourite"

Gerald Coulson

WINTER SUNLIGHT

A very careful placing of the vanishing point, the magnificent line of elms, and the church tower isolate and emphasise the single figure that is the central point of the composition. A low horizon and the dominating areas of sky and trees emphasise the largeness of nature and the smallness of man. Those with retrievers may muse on the placing and attitude of the dog (from the dog's point of view, of course, he's still practically at heel and the morning has not yet begun).

QUIET FOREST

Gerald Coulson's animal portraits are not numerous, but they display the same meticulous eye for detail, and sympathy with form and texture as any other of his subjects. The tenseness, like a taut spring, the defensive leap that one feels is imminent, implicit in the attitude of this magnificent stag could have been captured by very few artists. Indeed, most would finish up with a Landseer or a whisky advertisement. Or both.

Her name, actually, is *Princess Royal* and she is a Burrell 2879 engine. The original Charles Burrell of Thetford in Norfolk showed his first engine in 1848 and the company was well into its stride as a major producer by the time this engine left the works on 5 February 1907. Registered as No 698, she is a double crank, compound, spring-mounted showman's road locomotive, with the front-mounted dynamo, characteristic of all this type of engine, on its platform. Sold originally to Dawson Brothers at Boston, Lincolnshire, she is now owned by E.W. Gale of Whittlesea, Northamptonshire. This rich study of the *Iron Lady* in all her carefully restored showman's glory was one of the first Coulson prints from Frost and Reed and laid the foundation of his future reputation.

IRON LADY

GREAT WESTERN EXPRESS

The main text (p22) covers this picture in some detail. The Great Western railway introduced the 4-6-0 locomotive as their standard heavy passenger engine, Collett designing the King class in 1927. No European 4-6-0 ever exceeded their 40,300lb tractive effort and they regularly clocked the magic 100mph. With a 23 ton axle loading and a capability of hauling an 800-ton train, it was sheer weight and not only the extra-broad coaches that restricted them to the Bristol, Birmingham and Plymouth main lines.

Hot sun glares down upon the aircraft cruising serenely among the developing cumulus with their thrusting thunderheads — the 'mumblies' — unfolding. The Mk I Spitfire belongs to No 610 (County of Chester) Squadron, Royal Auxiliary Air Force.

LONE SPITFIRE (I)

BLACK LABEL BENTLEY

This print has also been extensively discussed in the main text (pp23-4). A static, rather than dynamic rôle for the car has been chosen, its massive dignity very much to the fore in this formal portrait — an interesting choice, considering the enormous vigour of the two railway prints. Apart from a series for a French calendar, this is the only motor car Gerald Coulson painted.

BRISTOL BULLDOG

This was the first aviation print made by Coulson for Frost and Reed, and followed a number of earlier paintings on similar lines. As one of his 'development' works, it has been described in some detail in the text (p22).

HAWKER FURY

It has already been mentioned that Gerald considered the Hawker Fury to be one of the most beautiful aircraft, and it was a subject that he came back to several times. The first occasion on which he tackled it was for the Frost and Reed series of prints to complement the Bulldog, and he has shown one of No 43 Squadron's immaculate aircraft in all its glory of highly polished aluminium, silver-doped fabric and the black-and-white chequered squares that were 43's heraldic device.

It was built round Rolls-Royce's classic V-12 Kestrel engine, which was small enough to let Sidney Camm design an elegantly slim fuselage round it, yet powerful enough to give the Fury a decent performance as an interceptor fighter with a top speed of 207mph and a rate-of-climb that took it to 10,000 feet in 4½ minutes. Camm gave it very sensitive controls and it was a magnificent aerobatic mount, adored by every pilot that flew it.

No 43 Squadron was the first to receive the Fury, at Tangmere, in the summer of 1931, and hung on to them until the end of 1938 when it began to exchange them for the big, sombre Hurricanes that it took to war. This particular Fury, K2050, was from the second batch of forty-eight, built by Hawker Aircraft Ltd and delivered in early 1932. It had an adventurous career, serving with Nos 1, 25 and 43 Squadrons and Nos 5 and 8 Flying Training Schools, before being transferred to the South African Air Force on 5 August 1940.

TRAWLER LEAVING FRASERBURGH HARBOUR

An interesting Coulson, this: an unusual subject, because he is not a marine artist by nature, and a technique which is quite different from the smooth quality of most of his landscapes. The composition, too, has its moments; the lighthouse and trawler both anchored (so to speak) to the very centre of the picture, and the strong vertical of the clouds between the two very powerful verticals of the lighthouse itself and the mast and funnel of the trawler.

BLACKFRIARS BRIDGE

Like *Trawler Leaving Fraserburgh Harbour,* this is an unusual Coulson. Architectural landscapes, like ships, are not frequent products of his brush. He has chosen a slightly cold, impersonal atmosphere for this painting of the Thames, an impersonality heightened by the comparative lack of movement, apart from the inevitable police launch and the (equally inevitable) seagulls. Quite the most exciting thing in the composition is the magnificent lamp standard, right up against the edge of the picture and providing the necessary weight to balance the increasing bulk of buildings towards the left-hand edge.

HAY LOADING

One of the richest and most satisfying of the Coulson landscapes. This time the sky is not allowed to dominate the structure as it does in so many of his paintings. The horizon line is fairly high and the clouds themselves are muted in design, providing a backdrop rather than a major element. Reinforced by the pattern of water in the foreground, all attention is concentrated in the three closely related and near-identical masses of the trees and the hay waggon. The horizon has been carefully chosen to put the horses' heads above it, against the sky, where they act as a focal point for the three main areas.

THE ANGLER

This is one of the busiest of all the landscapes. Plenty of exercise is provided for the eye, and it is a measure of the artist's skill that the intricate pattern of shapes formed by the tree in the foreground and the barrier of leafy branches in no way distract from the figure of the fisherman, to whom all the major lines of the composition inevitably lead. In addition the tonal perspective, particularly of the background trees which fade rapidly into obscurity, tends to the same result.

THE CHAFF CART

This is one of Coulson's most intriguing canvases. The main feature, the cart itself, is completely isolated from the rest of the picture. He has chosen an unusually elongated frame which emphasises the uncompromising horizon line, but in fact, a frame of almost any size or proportion would not have disturbed the main group. The rather gloomy effect of a completely empty landscape is avoided by the bush breaking the skyline. And, of course, another of those delightful dogs. Is he looking for Cuneo's mouse?

THAT MAGIC MOMENT

The influence of the late nineteenth century is clear in many of Gerald Coulson's landscapes, notably in his fidelity to the natural scene in all its detail. His ability to ring the changes in style, from his great sweeps of sky and water to these more intimate, formal pictures is remarkable. At the same time, his appreciation of the value of large, carefully contoured spaces prevents him from niggling at foliage, while his skills enable him to fill those larger segments of the design with a rich pattern of vegetation. In this case, in order to reinforce the feeling of the forest closing in round the central figure, the horizon has been lifted right out and the steep, tree-clad hills form the only backdrop.

THE PLOUGHMAN AND THE SEA

Ploughing those great clay uplands, you would need an early start to the day. You would also need the Shire horse — the Great Horse of England — whose origins go back over four hundred years (the plough appears to be contemporary with that date). Greys are comparatively rare among Shire horses, predominant colours being bay and brown. The early birds among the local gull population are already homing in on the breakfast worms turned up by the plough.

THE BIG SKY

Unlike *The Ploughman and the Sea,* the whole emphasis of this painting concentrates on the sky, with the hazy sun lighting the towering cumulus that has been building up through the afternoon, and the soft sunlight falling on the distant coast. Here the ploughman and his team of Shire horses are a less significant element, merely serving to break the monotony of the shoreline, while the seagulls provide a foreground note.

OUTBOUND LANCASTER
CROSSING THE EAST COAST

One of the most famous of all Gerald Coulson's paintings, reproduced as a fine art print by Solomon and Whitehead and displaying all the hallmarks of his simple composition and meticulous attention to detail.

THE SINKING OF THE *TIRPITZ*

The wretched *Tirpitz* was the last example of the theory of the 'fleet in being', whereby a ship's mere presence — sometimes without her even putting to sea — locked up powerful enemy forces to contain her threat: thus *Tirpitz* skulked about the coast of Norway for nearly three years while repeated attempts to eliminate her met with only partial success. Finally, on 29 November 1944, she moved within range of the specially modified Lancasters of Nos 617 and 9 Squadrons. Using the 12,000lb armour-piercing bombs introduced four months earlier, they sank her with three hits and two near misses. The painting was commissioned by Rolls-Royce for presentation to the RAF College, Cranwell.

OVERDUE

For the first half of the war, the sturdy Wellington was the mainstay of Bomber Command and it continued in front-line service until the end of hostilities. By the end of 1941 there were thirty-one squadrons equipped with them, and 599 of the 1,000 bombers that attacked Cologne on 30 May 1942 were Wellingtons. On 18 December 1939, aircraft from Nos 9, 37 and 149 Squadrons repeated the raid made in September by Blenheims on the German fleet, though they lost ten out of twenty-four aircraft. A 149 Squadron Wellington dropped the first 4,000lb bomb on Germany. In the painting a crippled Wellington, limping home after a raid and barely holding its height above the cold and uncharitable sea, drives its lonely way back towards sanctuary.

LOW LEVEL STRIKE — 1943
de Havilland Mosquito B. Mk. IV

A magnificent, classic Coulson ('The Master of the Single Vanishing Point') with two Mosquitos, lovingly drawn with every care for their exquisite lines, racing home at low level from their target which can be seen, bomb-shrouded and shaken, in the far distance.

DAWN

Another demonstration of the advantages of composing one's own landscape; it would be hard to believe that all the elements in this peaceful scene had been so arranged by nature. Three sets of parallel, interlocking curves define the foreground, middle distance and horizon, cut by the strong horizontal of the far river bank. Emphasised neatly by the gap in the trees, the solitary figure, frequently used by Coulson, fishes happily.

DUSK

Painted as a companion piece to *Dawn,* this outstanding landscape has qualities that set it a little apart from other Coulson works. The sheer intensity of the mood created by the masterly handling of the sunset sky and the solitary line of melancholic clouds is emphasised by the total lack of any human activity. It is a mood inspired, one might feel, as much by nineteenth-century novelists as by their contemporary painters. The general impression is heightened, rather than dissipated, by the distant church, framed between the trees in its own patch of clear evening light. The similar areas of the two reflecting lights on the water help to draw attention back from this evidence of man to the general wildness of the landscape, while repetition of the tower-shape in other places along the horizon fills a similar function.

An interesting composition, with the parallel verticals of the barge's masts and the right-hand edges of cloud, wood and boat, the latter dividing the quiet trees from the action, and the boat, the centre of interest, passing from inaction to action. The weed-covered shore in the foreground turns back the eye and forms an anchor to the triangle with boat and barge. Very careful composition inevitably marks Coulson's work and adds unconscious excitement to his peaceful landscapes.

EARLY START

Another Coulson classic: the solitary wayfarer on the receding road and the splendid portraits of the trees, with all the artist's skills employed to convey the sharp air of the frost-bound landscape. The dog seems singularly uninterested in the rocketing pheasant, but the latter is patently taking no chances.

FROSTY MORNING

MYSTÈRE

BRISTOL 188

Avions Marcel Dassault is one of the great survivors of the French aircraft industry; an industry where, for various reasons over the years, not many *have* survived at all. When the 1937 nationalisation programme grouped all military building into State-controlled groups, Marcel Dassault was fortunate in that he was building civil as well as military aircraft, and kept a measure of independence. Incidentally he was Marcel Bloch then, but thought it sounded too German and changed it. After the war Dassault began designing, building and selling a long series of extremely successful fighters: the straight-wing Ouragan, swept-wing Mystère and the current Mirage series, most of which are deltas. Dassault teamed up with Louis Breguet's company in the most recent rationalisations and is now Avions Marcel Dassault-Breguet Aviation (AMD-BA), but more commonly Dassault-Breguet. This is the earliest Coulson available for reproduction, dating from 1955, and so of considerable interest. It is also the only watercolour of his of which a record is available. All the features for which he was to become famous are there: the careful blending of cloud, aircraft and contrail to emphasise movement, and the meticulous accuracy of drawing.

Advertising material inevitably demands a more dramatic presentation than a normal painting, and the artist has responded very well in this case. Among other problems that face anyone designing a painting for this purpose is the awkwardness of having to work to a portrait layout of slightly daunting proportions — as well as having to provide 'unoccupied' space for the various headings and printed matter. The result, in this case, was extremely striking — and it was nobody's fault, as far as painter and advertiser were concerned, that the aeroplane, when built, turned out to be a flop.

THE LONELY SKY

Somehow, the tranquillity and the sense of human isolation that nearly always pervade the Coulson landscapes never fail to appear in the skyscapes of his aviation work. He is not a man for battle, murder and sudden death. This Royal Aircraft Factory S. E. 5A, high in the sunlit silence and wrapped in the vastness of the air, is no exception. The S. E. 5A was designed at Farnborough by Frank Godden, the last Royal Aircraft Factory design to reach the Royal Flying Corps before the Factory was told to get back to its primary task of research. Unlike their abysmal death-wish two seaters, the S. E. 5A was a good design, and in the hands of pilots like Ball, McCudden and Mannock it was a very successful fighting machine.

MOMENT OF TRIUMPH

The 'moment', of course, was the final outright winning of the fabulous Schneider Trophy by the Royal Air Force High Speed Flight in 1931. The aircraft was the Supermarine S. 6B, the ultimate expression in a line of racing seaplanes designed by Reginald Mitchell, who would take the experience this exercise in modern, metal, high-speed aircraft gave him, to create the Spitfire. Shortly after the event, the S. 6B raised the world air speed record to a staggering 407mph.

Here the aircraft, in the hands of Flt Lt Boothman, is seen hurtling round the Solent course, a mark boat destroyer in the distance and the Hampshire shore on the horizon.

BIRTH OF A LEGEND

There are very good grounds for asserting that this is Coulson's finest aviation painting yet. The classical beauty of the uncluttered prototype Spitfire, gleaming in its special paint, has been caught to perfection. All the artist's training and skill in technical drawing, his meticulous attention to detail, and his profound interest in his subject have come together to produce a portrait displaying every ounce of the character of the original. The prototype Spitfire, conforming to Air Ministry Specification F. 37/34, flew for the first time on 5 March 1936 with a Rolls-Royce Merlin 'C' engine and fixed-pitch, two-bladed wooden airscrew, achieving 346mph. It was eventually brought up to full Service standard, but crashed at Farnborough on 4 September 1940 and was not, apparently, rebuilt.

OFF DUTY — LANCASTER AT REST

This delightful study of a Lancaster in one of its quieter moments should really be classed as a landscape-with-aircraft in the traditional early morning style, rather than a painting of an aircraft. Judging by the presence of the 'Trolley, Accumulator', better known as the 'trolleyacc.', the Lancaster may not be at rest for much longer.

LAST QUIET MOMENT

Where are they going, this Stirling crew taking their last relaxing cigarette before the start-up, the take-off and the long grind to the target? Over the Alps to Turin? Back into 'Happy Valley', the heavily defended Ruhr? For the Stirlings, lower and slower than the other four-engined bombers, there were certainly few quiet moments once the night's work had started. This is good, vintage Coulson, the more interesting for his handling of (for him) an unusual subject.

HAPPY DAYS

East Anglia is an ideal area for low flying, and more than one owner or operator of a Tiger Moth in that part of the world indulges himself quietly in a little bending of the rules. What the Air Navigation Order actually forbids is flying within 500 feet of any person, animal or structure; you don't necessarily have to be 500 feet up in the air. And anyway, who is the rabbit going to complain to?

THE FIRST BLOW

This dramatic picture was painted to commemorate the fiftieth anniversary of the first RAF raid of World War II, an attack on German warships anchored in the Schillig Road. It was made by fifteen aircraft from Nos 107 and 110 Squadrons from Wattisham and 139 from Wyton. Despite glowing accounts in the press at the time, results were in fact poor, and half the attacking force were shot down. The raid was led by Flt Lt Doran and took place on 4 September 1939; the previous day a 139 Squadron Blenheim from Wyton, flown by Flighing Officer Macpherson, was the first British aircraft across the German frontier, taking photographs. Both officers were gazetted simultaneously on 10 October for the DFC, the first decorations won by the RAF in World War II.

SILENT MAJESTY

In this painting, the artist has deliberately divided the attention equally among the elements of the design, giving equal weight to the single beast, the landscape and the trees, and the great snow-capped mountains hanging distantly over the whole scene. To what does the title refer? We are thus given a small diversion, a focus outside the picture itself, to exercise our minds, as we are in *Friendly Persuasion* (p64).

The most striking things about this dramatic picture are firstly, the almost violent clash of the warm colours of the foreground and the ominous greys of the approaching storm, the effect, of course, serving to heighten the drama; and secondly, the immensely rich texture of the painting of the load and the ground, and of the great rolls of cumulus and cumulo-nimbus, sailing solidly across the sky.

THE GATHERING STORM

The figures busily engaged around the horse and cart and the happily fossicking dog serve to balance the intricate pattern of the tree on the left, but they are no more than ancillary notes to the great sweep of the evening sky and the tranquil sheet of water. The balance of elements in this painting is very much in line with the artist's views on priorities in landscapes.

EVENING HARVEST

FRIENDLY PERSUASION

For once, the major constituents of these calm and tranquil landscapes are not the masses of sky and countryside, of water and trees, but the sheepdog and the lamb in the foreground which are acting out the caption. Reminiscent of the aviation paintings is the violent recession of the line of sheep, leading the eye into the picture to the solitary figure, dark against a light background — yet another characteristic of the artist's work. Interesting, too, is the solid texture of the sky, giving it very much the same weight as the distant hills, and sharply limiting recession.

There is a faint echo of the Renaissance in this centrally balanced mood picture — one feels that Piero di Cosimo would regard it with a benevolent eye. The mood is set by numerous repetitions of shape, giving a wholly static air to the painting, relieved by the idle boat and the sole piece of action, the seagull rounding in to a vertical landing.

TRANQUILLITY

Torn for once from his favourite times of day, the artist gives full value to the rich lighting on the foliage and the detail on the boat. Aerial perspective still separates out the background as a single, flat plane and the parallel treatment of the cloud is interesting; flat, vertical, two-dimensional shapes on two planes, near and far. The very carefully arranged pattern of mast and sails is worth attention.

SHARING THE MOMENT

FORTRESS FORMATION

All the Coulson skills are well deployed for this gleaming Flying Fortress, evidently with delivery mileage only and none of the weathering caused by long hours in the air and the effects of an English summer. Boeing B-17G-BO 339109 carries the code letters of the 511th Bombardment Squadron, 351st Bombardment Group, 8th Air Force, United States Army Air Force. Camouflage was deleted on production B-17s from January 1944; the tail markings are those of the Group, the basic letter-triangle emphasised by the red band for recognition purposes. Assigned to 1 Bombardment Division, 94 Combat Bombardment Wing, the Group was based at Polebrook. Clark Gable flew missions with the 351st.

THUNDER AND LIGHTNINGS

This magnificent pair, Firestreak-equipped, just about to rotate at the critical point of a burner take-off, thrusting out of the storm that has soaked the runway, are Coulson drama at its best. The markings are those of No 111 Squadron in the early 1960s: on the fin, the official squadron badge bearing the cross to symbolise its World War I career in Palestine; the heraldic seaxes of Essex, where it was later based; and the red swords for the City of London, which it helped to defend. Black was the colour of the pre-war squadron marking. The lightning flash symbolised equipment with that aircraft.

SYNCHRO

One of the most breathtaking manoeuvres performed by the Red Arrows — the Royal Air Force aerobatic display team — is the cross-over of the synchro pair, performed several times in different configurations in the course of their programme. From this startling and unusual canvas, as the two Hawks cross in knife-edge flight, scant feet apart and at a closing speed of around 700 knots, it may be imagined that the dramatic quality of the pass is not entirely in the eye of the beholder. Reflected in the panoramic mirrors on the cockpit frame the pilot can see his own wing tips.

RED ARROWS

In the course of the hundreds of shows they put on each year, the Red Arrows team quite frequently finds itself performing away from an aerodrome, at a site such as the Dartmouth estuary in this picture. In the absence of a long runway that provides a positive reference for manoeuvres and positioning, that little bit more care is essential to align the performance about the datum point. The artist has therefore chosen to underline the attitude of the team in a vertical climb by rotating the horizon — as he has in the other Arrows painting, *Synchro.*

HUNTER'S MOON

One of the latest Coulson paintings to be created as a limited edition fine art print; it was completed early in 1990, with all his mastery of light and cloud surrounding the night-fighting Hurricane of No 85 Squadron. The squadron marking, a white hexagon forming part of their official unit badge, is a replica of the markings borne by the unit in World War I; the official identifying codes were VY. Coulson has again placed the aircraft in the centre of the painting, triangulated with the moon and its reflection, and reinforcing the static mood, hanging in the clear night air.

LONG NIGHT AHEAD

The setting for this lonely Lancaster, as it starts out for Europe and all the fury of the German defence, constitutes one of the most striking and magnificent sky paintings the artist has ever produced. Around half of the 7,374 Lancasters built were lost, nearly all to enemy action.

THUNDER IN THE HILLS

When the Tornado GR1 came into service, it replaced the Jaguars serving with Strike Command in the UK and with RAF Germany, except for a solitary squadron in each area dedicated to tactical reconnaissance. In the UK this unit was No 41 Squadron, and in Germany No 2. Like its namesake, Jaguar is fast and dangerous and operates *ventre à terre* in order to survive, and the artist has shown these 2 Squadron aircraft in a typical Jaguar setting: low down over the surface of the water, the dispersed pair take every advantage of terrain, speed and very low altitude to practise the evasion of enemy defences — a prime requisite for survival. The two white triangles on a black bar either side of the unit badge conform to fighter marking practice, and were also borne on the reconnaissance Swifts and Hunters of the squadron, as well as their Jaguars, at their Laarbruch base. Despite this, No 2 has always performed army co-operation and reconnaissance duties and carries the knot of Hereward the Wake on its badge as a reminder of its military duty.

For nearly four years the Mosquito was the fastest aircraft in RAF service; as a bomber, it remained the fastest until the Canberra arrived in 1951. The first bomber version (the Mk IV), carrying 2,000lb of bombs at up to 380mph, began to replace Blenheims in No 2 Group from November 1941. A private venture by de Havilland, drawing on A.E. Hagg's design experience with the Albatross airliner, it was built of wood — which did not have to be imported — and even though unarmed, was fast enough to enjoy the lowest loss ratio in Bomber Command.

DE HAVILLAND MOSQUITO MK IV

Gerald Coulson regarded the Hawker Fury biplane, quite rightly, as one of the most handsome aeroplanes in the world. Everything that he had learned from his growing experience about the painting of light reflected from burnished and polished metal, and about scrupulously painted and cleaned silver-doped fabric, has gone into this portrait of the Fury II, produced for Solomon and Whitehead some twenty years after the Fury I picture. The superbly sculptured Mk II had 20 per cent more power than the Mk I, with 8 per cent increase in speed and a staggering 34 per cent improvement in rate-of-climb. K7270 is shown in the markings of No 25 Squadron, first to receive the Mk II and based at Hawkinge in Kent. The Commanding Officer, S/Ldr Down, AFC, has his flag on the fuselage and the fin is in the squadron colour.

HAWKER FURY II

FEEDING THE GULLS

The way in which the horizontal planes of water and valley floor relate to the intersecting verticals of the mountains is interesting, but the most notable features are the foreground sky reflection and the rocks in the water, leading in to the brightly highlighted figures, and their relation to the carefully placed seagull, bracketed by the two clumps of trees. Minute in scale compared with the great masses of the landscape, they nevertheless successfully dominate the painting.

MILL IN THE MIST

In its outrageous simplicity of design and its trick of switching attention from the bulk and the busyness of the mill to the swift shapeliness of the duck (a fine pair of *Anas platyrhychos)*, this has to be one of the most satisfying of all Coulson's landscape paintings.

'From the mountains, moors and fenlands, Where the heron, the Shuh-Shuh-Gah, Feeds among the reeds and rushes' (Longfellow, *The Song of Hiawatha* — what else?). Here the classic Coulson riverside scene has been dramatised by the shafts of sunlight that burst out from behind the tree.

SILENT SENTINEL

One would wish to see more Coulson bird paintings. In the massive, snow-covered mountains that comprise its habitat across Europe and Asia, this wide-ranging raptor, hunting for the sparse food the area provides as far as 25 miles from its nest, dominates the landscape as he does the picture. The 'unlicensed aviator' here is *Aquila chrysaetos,* the great Golden Eagle.

UNLICENSED AVIATOR

INTO BATTLE

Lifting flatly off the ground at their 'best speed' climb, these two Hurricanes of No 32 Squadron scramble from Biggin Hill, participants in the preliminary fighting before the Battle of Britain got under way. GZ-H/N2532 was lost on 20 July that year and replaced as 'H' by P3522. The squadron hung on to their Hurricanes for a long time, not relinquishing them until the end of the summer of 1943. GZ-V is most probably P3757.

HURRICANE TRIO

Heading east in the late afternoon sunlight, these Hurricanes of No 501 (County of Gloucester) Squadron, Royal Auxiliary Air Force, are patrolling just above the scattered cloud around 'Angels two-zero' or 20,000 feet. The high horizon and the pale shafts of sunlight, obscuring the dimly seen earth below, all help to convey the feeling of altitude. After service in France, the squadron fought with No 11 Group in the Battle of Britain and kept their Hurricanes until April 1941. In the painting they are still holding the over-tight formation that was a legacy of pre-war fighting tactics; furthermore one of the aircraft, L2054 SD-E, crashed in France on 12 May 1940, which dates the picture nicely.

THE LAST PATROL

No 201 Squadron (originally 'Naval One' until the army and navy flying corps emerged to become the RAF in 1918) was flying Sunderland Vs towards the end of the war, having resumed its codes in July 1944. Circling one of the vast convoys — little troubled by U-boats, thanks to air and sea escort at the end of the war — the big boat against the setting sun symbolises the endless patrols of Coastal Command. The squadron retained its Sunderlands after the war, taking part in the Berlin airlift and being one of the last two units to stand down in January 1957. Sunderlands were the only RAF aircraft to fly operationally in the Korean war.

CAMBRIDGE AIRPORT 1938

The aviation career of Sir Arthur Marshall, OBE, DL, 1929-89

There is probably no man so widely revered within the aerospace industry and so little known outside it — apart from in his native Cambridgeshire — as Sir Arthur Marshall. His career spanned seventy-seven years, over sixty of them in the aircraft business, and when he retired (a trifle nominally, to be sure) at the end of 1989, Gerald Coulson, who had, of course, worked for him for several years, was commissioned to paint a suitable presentation picture. It took a long time to find the right formula, but when he did, it was a tremendous success. To quote Sir Arthur himself: 'When I look at the painting, I'm standing on the aerodrome, watching the aircraft fly past.'

There are twenty-five aircraft, including three on the ground (and an Austin Seven); some of the types with which Sir Arthur has been associated in his long business life. They are: TriStar, Concorde, Gulfstream III, Citation II, Canberra B6, Valiant, Viscount, Victor, VC 10, Hercules, Ambassador, Mosquito, Vampire T11, Whitley, Albemarle, B-17, Oxford, Rapide, Miles Falcon, Tiger Moth, Puss Moth, Gipsy Moth, Hart and Monospar. Readers may amuse themselves by the correct identification of each type.

FIREBIRD

The firebird is, of course, the phoenix, and the phoenix is the badge of No 56 Squadron, one of the most famous units in Royal Flying Corps and Royal Air Force history. The first squadron to receive the SE 5, it numbered among its members two VCs, Ball and McCudden, and also Rhys-Davids, who shot down the German ace Werner Voss. In Wold War II it was the first to get the Typhoon — a slightly dubious honour — and in 1954 was the first and only squadron to receive the Swift in its fighter form — an even more dubious honour. The Lightning came along in 1961 and XP701 is a Mk 3: the painting shows it with afterburners alight and wing shrouded in typical vapour blink as it tears through the humid air, and this must have been in 1966 or later, when the gaudy individual paint schemes had been replaced by official markings. No 56 had particularly colourful markings on its Lightnings, engendered by its rôle as the RAF aerobatic team, 'The Firebirds'.

CONCORDE

Concorde, that most emotive of aircraft, has roused more passionate argument both for and against it, than any other aeroplane in history yet it has been seen for many years of service as a triumph of the British and French aerospace industries. Gerald Coulson has painted it in the assured tranquillity of its high altitude cruise, poised against the vast bowl of the sky, while at the same time proclaiming in its attitude the supersonic urgency of its passage.

NIGHT INTRUDER

Like the Beaufighter, the Mosquito was as effective at night as by day, and here the artist shows the start of a Mosquito night intruder sortie, silhouetted by the last remnants of sunset. Fighter versions of the Mosquito — like their opposite number, the versatile Junkers Ju 88 — carried the war to the enemy by unnerving attacks on bomber airfields, catching tired and unwary crews in their home circuit.

NORMANDY SUNRISE

The Typhoon was designed before such aerodynamic advances as the laminar-flow wing were appreciated, and consequently never had the performance for its chosen rôle as an interceptor fighter; it found its true place in history as a ground-attack aircraft with bombs and rockets. Typhoons became famous for 'train-busting' operations in 1943, and were a major factor in getting the British army out of its bridgeheads in the summer of 1944, establishing remarkable 'sharpshooting' techniques to destroy German armour and soft-skinned vehicles; they managed to wipe out the 1st SS Panzer Division on 7 August at Mortain, among other successes. Rapid movement across Europe by the Allies meant the RAF was obliged to operate out of temporary landing grounds, and Gerald Coulson has caught one of the twenty-six Typhoon squadrons moving out for the first sortie of a busy day. All the wide-legged, brutal force of this big aircraft is convincingly portrayed against the omnipresent Normandy dust as they taxi out; reminiscent of 'Beef to the heels like a Mullingar heifer' as the chorus line in a Dublin music hall was once described.

HIGH STAKES

One of Gerald Coulson's comparatively rare still lifes is this study of the world's most famous revolver in what might be considered an appropriate setting — alongside playing cards and whisky. Depending on the nature of his opponent's hand and temperament, the man who drew these cards might well have also drawn the Colt, just to make sure. Samuel Colt's 'Single Action Army' pistol was adapted in 1873, the civilian model being known as the 'Peacemaker', or later as the 'Frontier Six-Shooter'. In spite of being a bit cumbersome and prone to breakages, it was immensely popular, partly because whatever broke, you could still fire the thing one way or another, and partly because it was so well-balanced that whatever you pointed it at, you tended to hit. It had an astonishingly long life, nearly 360,000 being made up to 1941, and in the wake of John Wayne Westerns and a craze for 'quick-draw' competitions, went back into production in 1955. The cards are probably by Andrew Dougherty of New York, and the whisky is anonymous but looks drinkable.

MALLARD

One of three railway subjects by the artist, the thunderous passage of this LNER main line express has given him the ultimate excuse to nail down the single vanishing point, his instinct for good composition and skilful brushwork retaining the dramatic onrush of the train without becoming banal. *Mallard* was a streamlined Gresley A4 Pacific 4-6-2 built for the London and North Eastern Railway, for their Anglo-Scottish services. The streamliners appeared in 1935, thirty-five being built, and before the war named trains such as *Coronation* and *Silver Jubilee* were run, reaching speeds of over 100mph as standard performance. The first of the class, No 2509 *Silver Link*, reached 112mph on its first trip. It and the next three engines were finished in silver for the *Silver Jubilee* trains, the others — including *Mallard* — being in Garter blue. The A4s remained in service until 1962 and pulled tremendous loads, including the 420-ton *Elizabethan* service non-stop between London and Edinburgh at an average 60.5mph. No 4468 *Mallard* set a record for steam trains in July 1938, of 126mph, and this is the subject of the painting.

It is interesting to note how many of the animal painters of the past have only ever portrayed the big cats in sombre, contemplative and placid moods: Bary, Guyot and Jouvre in the nineteenth century, Margat and Trémont in the twentieth; probably the result of painting at the zoo after feeding time. Even Géricault's delightfully vocal leopards are only 'playing at tigers and frightening nobody'. Possibly only Surand — some of whose snarling beasts are truly frightening — really comes near to 'nature red in tooth and claw'. The Coulson tiger, however, is most magnificently at bay: whoever has disturbed him takes one more step at his peril, and every line of the crouching body suggests aggressive defence. If one were to risk one more quotation, it would have to be 'Nemo me impune lacessit'.

TIGER, TIGER

It would be easy to become flippant about this delightful study of two polar bears. The whole picture revolves round those two noses; not quite as dramatic as the famous fingers of God and of Adam on the Sistine Chapel ceiling, but placed with the same carefully considered effect.

POLAR RENDEZVOUS

Spitfire Gallery

LONE SPITFIRE (II)

This remarkable painting, issued as a limited edition print by Solomon and Whitehead, is a considerable break from the rather placid view of nature normally taken by the artist. The sombre, dying light and the leaden clouds give an almost Gothic atmosphere to the scene, while the extravagant proportions of the frame emphasise the vastness of the horizon. There is an air almost of science-fiction in the effect.

PORTRAIT OF A THOROUGHBRED

A Spitfire Mk IXE of No 611 (West Lancashire) Squadron, Royal Auxiliary Air Force. One of the first Auxiliaries to receive the Spitfire, in May 1939, it flew the Mk IX from July 1942 for a year, reverting to the LF. VB for the next twelve months when the squadron exchanged its high-level patrol and escort work for low-level attacks with No 12 Group in preparation for D-Day — when it was the first squadron over the beachhead. It reverted to Mk IXs again for anti-shipping patrol in July, and later took part in DIVER operations against flying bombs. The handling of the aircraft in the painting is a technical masterpiece. (This picture was auctioned by Christie's on 28 April 1990, for £6,200.)

JOHNNIE COMES HOME

The period is 1943; the aircraft EN389, the Spitfire F Mk IXE of Wing Commander J.E. 'Johnnie' Johnson, who was to become the highest-scoring fighter pilot of the Royal Air Force in World War II, with at least 38 victories. Against an immensely satisfying and beautifully designed carpet of cloud, whose bold curving sweep echoes the track of the marginally off-centre aircraft, the back-lit Spitfire is a judicious mixture of bold areas of dark and light and of clear-cut detail that gives it identity and character. In 1943 W/Cdr Johnson, who survived the war and retired as an Air Vice-Marshal, was leading the first Canadian Wing from Kenley, in token whereof his aircraft carries a red maple leaf on a white disc below the windscreen. The codes are, of course, his initials (CO's perks). The aircraft has the recently introduced E wing with two 20mm cannon and provision for two .5 machine guns instead of four .303s.

IN THE SUNLIT SILENCE

No 92 Squadron is undoubtedly Gerald Coulson's favourite unit. In this painting, one of many commemorating the squadron's Spitfires, is portrayed a 'cooking' Mk 1A with eight machine-guns, this one painted during the summer of 1940 (the squadron pioneered the Mk IB with cannon and later became the first cannon-armed Spitfire squadron). Commanded by such famous Squadron Leaders as A. M. Maclachlan and 'Johnnie' Kent and based at Biggin Hill during the peak of the Battle of Britain, 92 was in one way remarkably conservative (or never read Air Ministry orders), for in the middle of the summer it was found to be still using its pre-war codes of GR.

GUARDIAN SPIRIT

The theme of the guardian spirit is a very old myth in military history, from Drake's Drum to the Angels of Mons (although Arthur Machen later admitted having made that one up out of whole cloth as an exercise in wartime propaganda). In this limited edition from Solomon and Whitehead, Gerald Coulson has taken the idea into World War II with a ghostly SE. 5A patrolling alongside a rather startled-looking Spitfire pilot, the misty distances and shrouded sun adding most effectively to the insubstantial atmosphere of the piece. The biplane ghost has been handled with great subtlety, with the slightest flush of colour on wing and wheel to add substance and the pilot clearly outlined. Between March and July of 1918, No 92 Squadron were based at Tangmere, with SE. 5As. In June 1940 they were at Hornchurch, flying Spitfire Is.

A PILOT'S VIEW

This painting was reproduced as a poster for the Imperial War Museum, Duxford, and used throughout the Underground stations of London in the spring of 1990; it might well therefore claim to be the best known Coulson of them all — except for the fact that the artist's name was lopped off. The late Roy Nockolds always considered that the most difficult and awkward of aviation subjects was a view from a cockpit; here it has been tackled with conspicuous success. Unexpectedly, the most time-consuming part of the research for this picture was finding reference for the Mk II gunsight. We are with No 92 Squadron, of course, heading for an apparently clear run at the bomber stream. At least there's nothing showing in the rear view mirror.

SOLITUDE

Not only Wordsworth 'wandered lonely as a cloud': *Solitude* also identifies this study of a No 19 Squadron Spitfire I. No 19 was the Service test unit for the Spitfire (the first to receive this type of aircraft), equipping at Duxford from the summer of 1938. The first one, K9798, arrived on 4 August, and the squadron was fully operational by the end of the year.

EVENING PATROL

QJ-P features in more than one of Coulson's Spitfire paintings. This time it is seen against one of the artist's evening skies, powerfully lit from the rear by the setting sun, in company with two of its fellows, QJ-N and QJ-D. 'P Peter' was N3249, later handed on to Nos 602 and 610 Squadrons and finally going missing on 14 February 1941.

HARVEST 1940

This is one of the 'action' Coulsons, a rare excursion into the fighting from the cloistered calm of *Solitude, Evening Patrol* and *In the Sunlit Silence.* The sharp recession to a central vanishing point, that Coulson uses so well to make his case, emphasises the swinging and triumphant rush of the Spitfire past its victim, while the distant hedgerows lead the eye round to the smoke rising from the target. The victim, a decidedly second-hand looking Heinkel He 111, sprawls 'like Ruth amid the alien corn', while its crew — one still wearing his padded kapok bomber life jacket — contemplate their opponent, a truly captive audience. The port engine has expired in a cloud of overheated coolant, and as the old advertisements used to say, 'Every Picture Tells a Story'.

SCRAMBLE!
The artist's contribution for the 50th Anniversary of the Battle of Britain

No 66 Squadron formed, or rather reformed, out of 'C' Flight, No 19 Squadron, at Duxford in 1936. Four years later it went through a similar gestation itself, giving birth to No 421 Flight (which later became No 91 Squadron) at Hawkinge. During the Battle of Britain period, in which this dramatic scramble scene is set, it flew Spitfire Is — in fact, it flew Spitfires continuously until 1947, when it converted to Meteors. The particular significance of this painting is that No 66 was at Coltishall from May to September, as was No 242, commanded by Douglas Bader and flying Hurricanes (seen taking off). Both units formed part of the Duxford 'Big Wing', propounded by No 12 Group Commander, Air Vice Marshal Sir Trafford Leigh-Mallory and enthusiastically supported by Bader. One of the few occasions that it actually worked was on 15 September, 'Battle of Britain Day'.

Index

Page numbers in *italics* indicate colour plates. Those in **bold** type indicate other types of illustrative material.